Tariffs
Taxes
&
Face Eating
Leopards

Also from EATMS Productions

Books on power, survival, women's autonomy, and the systems shaping modern America.

Nonfiction

Billionaires, Capitalism, and Power

Evil and the Mountain Ungreed
Self Help for American Billionaires
Selfish Steve and the Ivory Tower
Tariffs, Taxes, & Face-Eating Leopards
Ban Billionaires: Fascism Fix

Fascism, Religion, and Cultural Control

Self Help for the Manosphere
Fascism 2025
Fascism & the Perverts & the Greed Virus
Christian Fascism Marriage Book
Tyranny, Table Manners, & Tiramisu

Guides for Women's Autonomy and Protection

How to Survive in Post-America as a Woman
Project 2025 American Drag
4B – Burn, Ban, Boycott, Build
4B OG – So No Go GYN
I'm Glad He's Dead

Analysis of Authoritarian Project 2025

Project 2025: The Blueprint
Project 2025: The List
Project 2025, Christian Dumb Dumbs, & The Republican Agenda
Fascism, Project 2025, & The Pinkprint

Modern Rewrites for Women

Stoic Principles Reimagined
Siddhartha Reimagined
The Prince Reimagined for Women
The Art of War Reimagined for Women
The Jungle Reimagined
The Constitution Reimagined for Women

Machine Learning Series

AI, Bitcoin, Nostr for Women
AI, Safety, & Security for Women
AI, Anxiety, & Health for Women
AI, Kids, & Family Safety for Women
AI, Creativity, & Personal Expression for Women
AI, Independent Work, & Parallel Power for Women

Social Systems Series

Emotional Labor for Women
Household Power for Women
Workplace Power for Women
Medical Bias for Women
Aging Systems for Women
Recovery Systems for Women

Fiction

Dystopian Stories of Resistance and Collapse

Propaganda Paige & the Missing Prosperity
Propaganda Paige & the TIDE Manifesto
Propaganda Paige & the Shadow Cartographers
Propaganda Paige & the Prosperity Alliance
Propaganda Paige & the Shattered Truth
Propaganda Paige & the Rising TIDE
Propaganda Paige & the Last Bastion
Propaganda Paige & the Dawn of Prosperity
Project 2025: Dorian — The Last Men
Project 2025: Boy — A Last Men Novel

Tariffs
Taxes &
Face Eating Leopards

Capitalism v. Humanity1

by
Esme Mees &
Sandy van Tyne

EATMS
PRODUCTIONS

ISBN: 978-1-966014-09-6

Cover, interior design, interior prints by: Esme Mees

eatms@pm.me
www.eatms.me

Printed in the United States of America.

Never underestimate the power of stupid people in large groups.

— George Carlin

A tariff is a tax or duty imposed by a government on goods and services imported from other countries. It is designed to make foreign products more expensive, encouraging consumers to buy domestic alternatives and protect local industries. In theory, tariffs aim to create a level playing field by addressing trade imbalances or countering unfair practices like dumping, when foreign companies sell goods at artificially low prices to dominate a market. However, in practice, the cost of tariffs is often passed along the supply chain, ultimately raising prices for businesses and consumers. Far from being a straightforward economic tool, tariffs have complex ripple effects, influencing everything from global trade relationships to household budgets. When poorly designed, as was the case during Trump's administration, tariffs can act less as a shield for domestic industries and more as a stealth tax on the very people they are intended to protect.

A tax is a mandatory financial charge or levy imposed by a government on individuals, businesses, or other entities to generate revenue for public expenditures. Taxes are the primary way governments fund essential services such as infrastructure, healthcare, education, defense, and public safety. They can also be used to influence economic behavior, such as discouraging harmful activities (e.g., smoking through excise taxes) or promoting investment in certain areas (e.g., tax credits for renewable energy). Taxes come in various forms, including income tax (levied on earnings), sales tax (applied to goods and services), property tax (based on the value of owned property), and corporate tax (on business profits). In the case of tariffs, they function as a type of indirect tax applied specifically to imported goods. While taxes are often framed as a collective contribution to societal well-being, their distribution and impact can be uneven, disproportionately affecting certain groups, particularly when hidden in policies like tariffs, which shift the financial burden to consumers without clear accountability.

As it pertains to a tariff, a tax is a financial charge imposed by a government on imported goods and services entering a country.

This tax is levied at the border and is typically paid by the importer, often a business that brings in foreign products for resale or manufacturing. However, the cost of this tax does not stop with the importer. It is usually passed along the supply chain, resulting in higher prices for manufacturers, retailers, and ultimately consumers. Tariffs function as a form of indirect tax, with the primary intent being to make imported goods more expensive, encouraging consumers to buy domestically produced alternatives. While governments may use tariffs to protect local industries, generate revenue, or address trade imbalances, they are, in practice, a stealth tax that disproportionately affects consumers and small businesses. By raising the overall cost of goods, tariffs act as an economic penalty on everyday transactions, effectively functioning as a hidden tax on the public.

A leopard is a large, carnivorous cat belonging to the genus Panthera. Known for its striking coat covered in distinctive rosette-shaped spots, the leopard is one of the most versatile and adaptable of the big cats. Native to regions across Africa and Asia, leopards inhabit a wide range of environments, from dense forests to arid savannas and mountainous terrains. Leopards are solitary hunters, relying on stealth, speed, and strength to ambush prey, which can range from small rodents to large antelope. Their ability to climb trees and carry heavy prey into the branches is a hallmark of their adaptability, providing both protection from scavengers and a secluded place to feed. Despite their beauty and agility, leopards are apex predators, indifferent to the well-being of their prey, a characteristic that makes them an apt metaphor for unchecked greed or destructive policies.

In the context of this book, the leopard serves as a symbolic predator, relentless, opportunistic, and unbothered by the consequences of its feast, mirroring the economic and social impacts of policies like tariffs that prey on the vulnerable while enriching the powerful.

Table of Contents

Introduction
Face Eating Leopard Nation

Imagine, for a moment, a calm afternoon at your favorite park. You're seated on a bench, savoring a sandwich, when a leopard saunters up. Not just any leopard, a charismatic, well-dressed one with an oddly familiar orange hue to its fur. It leans in, purrs about "Making the Park Great Again," and promises you a future so spectacular that even the pigeons will have gold-plated breadcrumbs. Enthralled, you agree to feed it. After all, who doesn't want greatness? Fast-forward a few months: the leopard isn't just nibbling on breadcrumbs; it's devouring your entire lunch. Soon, it's eyeing your wallet, your shoes, and, why not, your face. And you? Well, you sit there, bleeding and bewildered, mumbling, "I didn't think it would eat *my* face."

Welcome to the United States under Donald Trump's tariff policies.

This book isn't just about leopards or even tariffs, though both are undeniably central players in this bizarre dinner theater we're living through. It's about how we, as a nation, collectively decided to hand over our economic lunchboxes to a man who convinced us he was protecting them. It's about how tariffs, those seemingly noble economic tools, became stealth taxes on the very people who cheered their arrival. And it's about why, despite the bloodied aftermath, we might still queue up to feed the leopard again.

To set the stage, let's demystify the star of this spectacle: tariffs. For those of you who didn't nod off in high school economics, tariffs are essentially taxes imposed on imported goods. The idea, in theory, is simple: charge foreign companies for selling their products in our market, making domestic goods more competitive. It's like charging your neighbor a toll for using your backyard swing set, hoping your own kids will finally play with the rickety seesaw you built. But as with most things that sound good in theory, tariffs in practice often create unintended consequences. When you tax imports, the costs get passed down the line, from foreign producers to domestic businesses to consumers. In other words, *you*.

Enter Donald Trump, a man who once declared, "I'm a tariff guy," as if that were an endearing personality trait rather than an ominous warning. Under Trump's economic vision, or what passes for one, tariffs weren't just tools; they were weapons. His trade wars, launched with all the subtlety of a cannonball into a teacup, targeted everyone from China to Canada. Yes, Canada, the land of maple syrup and Mounties, whose greatest offense was apparently being too polite.

Trump's tariffs were sold as a patriotic masterstroke, a way to wrestle America's manufacturing jobs back from the jaws of globalization. "China will pay the tariffs," he crowed repeatedly, as if tariffs were magical economic boomerangs that somehow skipped over American consumers. The reality, as economists patiently explained (to no avail), is that tariffs are paid by *importers*, who then raise prices on their goods to cover the cost. So when Trump slapped a tariff on Chinese steel, it wasn't China that footed the bill, it was American companies buying that steel, and by extension, American consumers buying the products made from it.

This brings us to the infamous $4,000 figure. According to experts, Trump's tariff policies would cost the average American household $4,000 a year. That's not chump change. That's a year of groceries, a semester of college tuition, or approximately 800 pumpkin spice lattes. But hey, who needs financial stability when you've got the satisfaction of knowing your imported goods are marginally less foreign?

To illustrate this absurdity, let's revisit our leopard. Imagine that every time you bought groceries, a leopard jumped out from behind the register and demanded a $50 surcharge. "It's for the good of the jungle," the leopard insists, as it pockets the cash and slinks off to its gold-plated lair. You're poorer, the leopard's fatter, and the jungle? Well, it's still a jungle.

But here's the kicker: Trump's tariffs weren't just a bad deal for consumers; they were a bonanza for the very corporations and industries they were supposed to protect. While American farmers watched their crops rot due to retaliatory tariffs from other countries, multinational corporations found clever ways to skirt the rules. Some shifted their supply chains to non-tariffed countries; others simply passed the costs onto consumers. Meanwhile, the Trump administration doled out billions in bailout money to struggling farmers, essentially paying them with taxpayer dollars to survive a crisis of its own making. Leopards don't just eat faces, it turns out; they also demand tips.

Now, you might be wondering: Could there have been a better way? Could we, perhaps, have avoided this gruesome buffet entirely? The short answer is yes. The long answer involves exploring non-tariff solutions like investing in domestic industries, negotiating fair trade agreements, and fostering innovation. You know, things that don't involve weaponizing taxes against your own citizens. But those approaches require nuance, collaboration, and an understanding of economics, all things that don't fit neatly onto a campaign slogan or a red baseball cap.

Here's the thing about leopards: they're predictable. You know exactly what they're going to do, and yet, there's something hypnotic about their charm. Trump's tariffs weren't an anomaly; they were a continuation of a long tradition of policies that masquerade as populist victories while quietly enriching the elite. It's socialism for the rich and rugged individualism for the rest of us, dressed up in the garb of economic patriotism. And the most maddening part? Many of us will cheer for the leopard again, convinced that this time, it'll leave our faces intact.

This book is not a dry policy analysis or a lecture on macroeconomics. It's a call to action, a wake-up slap for anyone still clinging to the belief that tariffs are anything but a stealth tax on the unsuspecting. It's a journey through the absurdities of Trump's economic policies, punctuated by the biting humor and sharp critique that only a good meme, and a sharp pen, can provide.

We'll explore how tariffs work (and don't), why they cost you more than you think, and what alternatives could actually make sense. Along the way, we'll revisit the leopard metaphor in all its grim hilarity, because sometimes, laughter is the only sane response to insanity.

So grab a snack, preferably one not subject to a 25% tariff, and settle in. It's time to meet the leopard, understand its appetite, and figure out how to keep your face off the menu. Spoiler alert: it starts by not voting for leopards.

Trump's First-Term Tariffs and Their Costs to Taxpayers

1.   Steel and Aluminum Tariffs (2018):

The U.S. imposed tariffs on imported steel and aluminum, costing American companies $5.1 billion. These tariffs raised production costs for manufacturers, which were ultimately passed down to consumers through higher prices on goods like cars, appliances, and construction materials.

2.   China Trade War Tariffs (2018-2020):

A series of tariffs on Chinese imports amounted to $81 billion in additional costs, which were largely absorbed by American consumers. These tariffs affected everyday items like electronics, clothing, and household goods, significantly straining household budgets.

3.   EU Retaliatory Tariffs (2018-2020):

In response to U.S. tariffs, the European Union imposed $7.5 billion in retaliatory tariffs, reducing revenue for American industries like agriculture and manufacturing. Exporters faced reduced demand, compounding economic losses.

4.   Farm Bailouts (2018-2020):

To offset losses from retaliatory tariffs, the U.S. government provided $28 billion in farm aid, funded entirely by taxpayers. This subsidy aimed to compensate farmers for declining exports but highlighted the economic damage caused by the trade war.

5.   Consumer Price Increases:

Across the board, tariffs led to price hikes on imported goods, costing the average American household between $200 and $500 annually in higher expenses. These increases affected everything from groceries to electronics, amplifying the financial burden on everyday consumers.

Chapter 1
Welcome to the Leopard Buffet

Part 1: The Leopard's Invitation

The concept of tariffs has long been dressed up as a noble economic tool, a strategic mechanism for shielding domestic industries and promoting national growth. But in practice, especially during Donald Trump's first term, tariffs became something far different, a blunt, erratic instrument wielded with all the precision of a sledgehammer at a symphony. The result wasn't harmony but chaos, a cacophony of economic fallout and unintended consequences that reverberated across every corner of American life. Yet, for all their complexity, tariffs are disarmingly simple in their effect. They are taxes, plain and simple, disguised as patriotism. And like any tax, the burden falls squarely on the shoulders of the people. In this case, the leopard metaphor is apt not just for its dark humor but for its brutal honesty. Leopards do what leopards do: they eat. And the tariff policies of the Trump administration were nothing more than an invitation to the leopards to feast, on wages, jobs, and ultimately, the financial security of the average American.

To truly understand the absurdity of Trump's tariff crusade, one must first grasp the economic mechanics behind it. Tariffs, at their core, are taxes on imports. When a government imposes a tariff, it's essentially charging foreign producers a fee for the privilege of selling their goods in the domestic market. In theory, this makes imported goods more expensive, encouraging consumers to buy locally produced alternatives. It sounds logical, even patriotic, but the reality is more nuanced. Foreign producers don't simply absorb the costs of tariffs; they pass them along, raising prices for domestic importers, who then raise prices for consumers. Every step of the supply chain absorbs a little of the cost until it reaches the end of the line, you, the buyer. This cascading effect transforms what was marketed as a penalty on foreign competitors into a stealth tax on everyday Americans.

When Donald Trump declared himself a "tariff man," he painted a picture of bold economic strategy. He promised that tariffs would rebuild American manufacturing, protect jobs, and level the playing field in international trade. To his supporters, it was a rallying cry, a way to stick it to foreign powers like China while reclaiming America's industrial dominance. What he didn't mention, or perhaps didn't understand, was that tariffs rarely deliver on these promises. Instead of fostering growth, they often stifle it, creating ripple effects that undermine the very industries they claim to protect. The steel and aluminum tariffs of 2018 are a case in point. Designed to bolster domestic metal producers, these tariffs raised costs for industries that rely on these materials, from car manufacturers to construction firms. For every job gained in steel production, several were lost elsewhere, as companies struggled to absorb the increased expenses.

The China trade war, Trump's pièce de résistance in tariff policy, showcased the full breadth of his economic misunderstanding. With a series of escalating tariffs on Chinese goods, he sought to punish Beijing for its trade practices, including intellectual property theft and currency manipulation. But instead of pressuring China into submission, the tariffs triggered a tit-for-tat escalation, with Beijing imposing retaliatory tariffs on American exports. U.S. farmers, once lauded as the backbone of the nation, found themselves caught in the crossfire, their crops piling up unsold as Chinese buyers turned to other markets. To mitigate the damage, the Trump administration rolled out a series of farm bailouts, totaling $28 billion. This was taxpayer money, mind you, funneled to farmers to offset losses created by a policy that was supposed to benefit them. It was an economic Ouroboros, a snake eating its own tail, except the snake was also asking you to foot the bill.

The costs didn't end there. Consumers bore the brunt of the trade war as prices for goods rose across the board. Everything from electronics to clothing became more expensive, with estimates suggesting that the average American household paid an additional $200 to $500 annually due to tariffs. For a middle-class family already grappling with stagnant wages and rising living costs, this was no small burden. And while Trump boasted that tariffs would bring jobs back to American shores, the reality was far more dismal. Companies, faced with higher production costs, either raised prices, cut jobs, or outsourced to countries not subject to tariffs. The promised resurgence of American manufacturing never materialized; instead, the trade war exacerbated economic inequalities, leaving the working class to bear the consequences of policies designed to help them.

Perhaps the most insidious aspect of Trump's tariff policy was the way it was sold to the public. Wrapped in the rhetoric of nationalism and economic empowerment, tariffs were framed as a way to "put America first." But what does it mean to put America first when the policies in question harm the very people they're supposed to help? The beneficiaries of Trump's tariffs were not the small businesses or blue-collar workers he claimed to champion but large corporations that found ways to game the system. Multinational companies rerouted their supply chains, sourcing goods from countries not subject to tariffs, while smaller businesses without such flexibility struggled to stay afloat. Once again, the leopard feasted not on the powerful but on the powerless, its appetite seemingly insatiable.

As the trade war dragged on, the cracks in Trump's strategy became increasingly apparent. Export-dependent industries suffered, with farmers, manufacturers, and even tech companies feeling the squeeze. The global economy, already fragile, teetered under the weight of uncertainty, as countries scrambled to adapt to the new trade landscape. And yet, despite the mounting evidence of its failures, the Trump administration doubled down, extending and expanding tariffs in a show of stubborn defiance. It was a textbook example of policy inertia, where the fear of admitting defeat outweighed the need for course correction. The leopard, having devoured its fill, was now gnawing on the bones, and still, the feast continued.

The legacy of Trump's tariffs is a cautionary tale, a reminder of the dangers of economic hubris and the allure of simple solutions to complex problems. Tariffs, when used judiciously, can be effective tools for addressing specific trade imbalances or protecting nascent industries. But when wielded recklessly, as they were under Trump, they become a blunt instrument, causing more harm than good. The leopard metaphor, with its dark humor and stark imagery, captures this dynamic perfectly. Leopards don't discriminate; they eat whatever is in front of them, whether it's a miscalculated economic policy or the unsuspecting public that voted for it. And as history has shown, once a leopard gets a taste for something, it's hard to stop it from coming back for more.

This is the world we were left with at the end of Trump's first term: a fractured global trade system, a domestic economy grappling with the fallout of self-inflicted wounds, and a populace divided not just politically but economically. The promise of tariffs as a path to prosperity had proven to be a mirage, an illusion of strength that masked deep structural weaknesses. And yet, the leopard waits, its appetite undiminished, ready for the next invitation to the table. The question now is not whether the leopard will return but whether we will have the wisdom to stop feeding it.

The first part of this chapter ends with that question, hanging heavy in the air. It's not just a question about tariffs or even Trump; it's a question about who we are as a nation and what kind of future we want to build. The leopard may be a metaphor, but the choices we face are very real. And as the next part of this chapter will explore, the path forward requires not just recognizing the mistakes of the past but finding the courage to chart a new course, one that prioritizes the needs of the many over the appetites of the few.

Part 2: Cleaning Up After the Leopard

If Part 1 is the grim spectacle of a leopard's feast, then Part 2 must focus on the aftermath, the wreckage left behind, the consequences ignored, and the choices ahead. The most haunting part of the leopard metaphor isn't that it eats your face; it's that after it's done, you're left wondering if it was your fault for feeding it in the first place. The Trump administration's tariff policies didn't just create immediate economic fallout; they exposed deeper systemic issues, many of which persist today. The leopard didn't just eat our faces, it took a chunk out of our collective confidence in trade, governance, and economic fairness. And yet, like victims of Stockholm syndrome, there remains a segment of the population eager to invite it back for another meal.

To understand why tariffs continue to hold appeal despite their glaring failures, we must examine the psychology behind them. Tariffs are, at their core, a simplistic solution to a multifaceted problem. They appeal to the human desire for immediate results, for a button we can press to fix what ails us. In the case of Trump's trade wars, the "problem" was framed as foreign exploitation of American markets, China stealing our jobs, Mexico undermining our industries, Europe taking advantage of our generosity. Tariffs were sold as a way to right these wrongs, to punish the perpetrators and restore balance. It's a narrative that resonates deeply in an era of economic anxiety, where the average worker feels increasingly powerless in the face of globalization and technological disruption.

But this narrative, like most populist rhetoric, is built on a foundation of half-truths and oversimplifications. Yes, globalization has created winners and losers, and yes, some foreign governments engage in unfair trade practices. But the idea that tariffs alone could reverse decades of economic shifts is a fantasy. The jobs that disappeared didn't vanish solely because of cheaper imports; they were automated away, offshored due to corporate decisions, or rendered obsolete by changing consumer demands. A factory town decimated by globalization won't be saved by a 25% tariff on Chinese goods. What it needs is investment in education, infrastructure, and new industries, solutions that are complex, long-term, and politically unsexy.

The failure to address these underlying issues is one of the great tragedies of Trump's tariff policies. Instead of using the trade war as an opportunity to invest in domestic resilience, the administration squandered billions on short-term fixes and political theater. The $28 billion in farm bailouts is a prime example. While these payments may have temporarily alleviated the pain for some farmers, they did nothing to address the root causes of the crisis. Worse, they reinforced a system where the government steps in to clean up the mess created by its own policies, effectively subsidizing the consequences of its own incompetence. It's a cycle as absurd as it is infuriating: create a problem, spend taxpayer money to mitigate the fallout, and then claim victory while ignoring the structural damage left behind.

This damage wasn't confined to the economy. Trump's tariffs also eroded America's global standing, undermining relationships with allies and emboldening rivals. The trade war with China, for instance, may have been intended to assert American dominance, but it had the opposite effect. By alienating key trading partners and destabilizing global markets, the tariffs created opportunities for China to strengthen its own trade networks. Countries that once relied on the U.S. for agricultural exports, like Brazil and Argentina, capitalized on the void left by retaliatory tariffs, establishing themselves as major suppliers to China. Meanwhile, U.S. farmers were left scrambling to regain lost market share, a task made even more difficult by the lingering uncertainty of trade policies.

The domestic consequences of this uncertainty cannot be overstated. For businesses, stability is everything. Companies need predictable conditions to make long-term investments in equipment, infrastructure, and workforce development. The chaos of Trump's trade policies, with their abrupt announcements and ever-shifting targets, created an environment where planning became nearly impossible. Manufacturers hesitated to expand operations, unsure if the next round of tariffs would upend their supply chains. Small businesses, already operating on razor-thin margins, struggled to absorb the rising costs of imported goods. Even consumers, whose spending drives the economy, became more cautious, wary of price hikes and economic instability.

This ripple effect extended beyond the immediate players in the trade war. Tariffs on goods like steel and aluminum impacted industries as diverse as construction, automotive, and aerospace, creating a cascade of higher costs that eventually reached the average worker. Consider the example of a construction company building a new apartment complex. The increased price of steel raises the cost of materials, which forces the company to either delay the project, cut corners, or pass the costs onto renters. In the end, it's not just the company that suffers, it's the people who can no longer afford a place to live. This is the true legacy of tariffs: a slow, insidious erosion of economic opportunity that leaves everyone worse off except for the leopard.

And yet, despite all of this, tariffs remain politically popular, particularly among certain segments of the population. Part of this can be attributed to the way they're marketed. Tariffs are framed not as taxes but as patriotic acts, a way to "stand up" to foreign adversaries and "protect" American jobs. This rhetoric taps into a deep well of national pride, appealing to the belief that America should never have to compromise or rely on others. It's a message that resonates especially strongly in communities that have been left behind by globalization, where the scars of factory closures and job losses are still fresh. For these voters, tariffs offer a sense of agency, a way to fight back against forces they feel powerless to control.

But this sense of empowerment is an illusion, a sleight of hand designed to distract from the real beneficiaries of tariff policies. While the public focuses on the symbolic victory of "making China pay," the corporations and wealthy elites who control the levers of the economy quietly reap the rewards. Multinational companies, with their vast resources and global reach, are better equipped to adapt to tariffs than the small businesses and workers they employ. They can shift production to non-tariffed countries, negotiate favorable terms with suppliers, or simply absorb the costs without significantly impacting their bottom line. Meanwhile, the workers and consumers who lack such flexibility are left to bear the brunt of the fallout.

This disconnect between rhetoric and reality is at the heart of the leopard metaphor. Leopards, after all, don't care about the well-being of their prey. They don't differentiate between those who voted for them and those who didn't. They eat indiscriminately, driven by hunger rather than loyalty. The same can be said of Trump's tariffs. For all the talk of protecting American interests, these policies served primarily to feed the insatiable appetite of a system that prioritizes profit over people. The leopard, in this case, isn't just a metaphor for the tariffs themselves, it's a symbol of the broader economic and political forces that perpetuate inequality under the guise of progress.

So where do we go from here? How do we break free from the cycle of feeding the leopard, only to be devoured in return? The answer lies not in abandoning trade altogether but in rethinking the way we approach it. Instead of using tariffs as a blunt instrument, we need policies that address the root causes of economic insecurity. This means investing in education and job training to prepare workers for the industries of the future. It means strengthening labor protections to ensure that workers receive a fair share of the wealth they create. It means pursuing trade agreements that prioritize cooperation over confrontation, recognizing that a globalized economy requires global solutions.

Above all, it means being honest about the limitations of tariffs and the complexities of the challenges we face. There are no easy answers, no silver bullets that can magically restore the past. But by acknowledging the mistakes of the past and learning from them, we can begin to chart a new course, one that prioritizes the well-being of people over the appetites of leopards. The road ahead won't be easy, but it's a journey worth taking. Because in the end, the only way to stop the leopard is to stop feeding it. And that starts with us.

Chapter 2
Feeding the Leopard – The Mirage of Tariffs

Part 1: The Tariff Mirage

In the years leading up to Donald Trump's presidency, America had already begun to grapple with the widening chasm between its economic rhetoric and its reality. The promises of globalization, cheaper goods, more jobs, and shared prosperity, had failed to materialize for vast swaths of the country. Instead, factory towns decayed, blue-collar workers were left stranded, and the dream of upward mobility began to feel like a cruel illusion. Into this fertile ground of disillusionment stepped Trump, armed with a simple and seductive narrative: the problem wasn't globalization itself but the unfair deals America had struck along the way. And the solution? Tariffs. Bold, unapologetic tariffs, aimed at punishing foreign competitors and restoring the greatness that had been stolen. It was a compelling mirage, shimmering with the promise of rebirth and renewal, but like all mirages, it masked the harsh desert of reality waiting just beyond.

To understand why tariffs held such appeal, one must first consider the emotional weight of economic betrayal. For decades, workers in the Rust Belt had been told that globalization would lift all boats, that the pain of job losses in the short term would be offset by gains in the long term. But the long term never arrived. Instead, factories closed, communities withered, and the wealth generated by international trade seemed to flow upwards rather than outwards. This left a deep scar on the American psyche, a sense that the system was rigged, that the promises of prosperity were nothing more than lies. Tariffs, in this context, offered not just an economic solution but an emotional one. They were a way to strike back, to reclaim dignity and agency in a world that seemed increasingly indifferent to the plight of ordinary people.

Trump understood this dynamic instinctively. His rallies were less about policy specifics and more about the performance of grievance and defiance. When he spoke about tariffs, it wasn't in the dry, technocratic language of economists but in the fiery rhetoric of a populist crusader. "They've been robbing us blind," he would declare, pointing the finger at China, Mexico, or any other convenient scapegoat. "Not anymore." The crowd, hungry for vindication, roared its approval. Tariffs weren't just taxes on imports; they were acts of retribution, a way to punish those who had exploited American goodwill. The simplicity of this message was its greatest strength, and its greatest weakness.

The problem with simplistic solutions is that they rarely hold up under scrutiny, and tariffs were no exception. The basic mechanics of a tariff are straightforward: by imposing a tax on imported goods, the government makes those goods more expensive, thereby encouraging consumers to buy domestic alternatives. In theory, this boosts domestic production and protects local industries from foreign competition. But in practice, the effects are far more complex and often counterproductive. When the Trump administration imposed tariffs on steel and aluminum in 2018, for example, it did succeed in boosting domestic production in those sectors. A handful of mills reopened, and a few thousand jobs were created. But these gains were dwarfed by the losses in downstream industries that rely on steel and aluminum, such as automotive manufacturing, construction, and appliance production.

The increased cost of imported metals rippled through the economy, raising prices for businesses and consumers alike. Car manufacturers, for instance, faced higher costs for raw materials, which they either absorbed, reducing profits, or passed on to consumers through higher prices. In a fiercely competitive market, neither option was sustainable. As costs rose, some companies were forced to cut jobs or delay investments, undermining the very economic growth the tariffs were supposed to generate. A study by the Peterson Institute for

International Economics found that for every job created in the steel and aluminum industries, eight jobs were lost elsewhere in the economy. These were not just numbers on a spreadsheet; they were lives disrupted, plans derailed, and communities further destabilized.

The trade war with China escalated these dynamics to a new level of dysfunction. Over the course of 2018 and 2019, the Trump administration imposed tariffs on hundreds of billions of dollars' worth of Chinese goods, targeting everything from electronics to textiles. The stated goal was to pressure China into changing its trade practices, particularly its policies on intellectual property theft and forced technology transfers. But instead of capitulating, China retaliated with tariffs of its own, targeting key American exports such as soybeans, pork, and aircraft. What ensued was a tit-for-tat escalation that plunged both economies into uncertainty and left countless businesses caught in the crossfire.

For American farmers, the impact was devastating. China had long been the largest buyer of U.S. soybeans, accounting for roughly 60% of all exports. When Beijing imposed a 25% tariff on American soybeans in response to Trump's actions, the market evaporated almost overnight. Farmers who had invested heavily in planting and harvesting found themselves sitting on unsold crops, watching their livelihoods crumble. To mitigate the fallout, the Trump administration announced a series of bailout packages, totaling $28 billion by the end of 2020. This was framed as a lifeline for farmers, but it came with its own set of problems. The payments were funded by taxpayers, effectively shifting the burden of the trade war onto the very people it was supposed to protect. And while the bailouts may have kept some farmers afloat, they did little to address the long-term damage. China, unwilling to rely on an unpredictable trading partner, began sourcing soybeans from Brazil and Argentina, relationships that would prove difficult to dislodge even after the tariffs were lifted.

The costs of the trade war were not limited to agriculture. Retailers, manufacturers, and small businesses across the country faced rising prices for imported goods, forcing many to make difficult decisions. Some companies managed to absorb the costs, cutting into already thin profit margins. Others raised prices, passing the burden onto consumers. And still others, unable to compete, closed their doors altogether. The human toll of these closures was immense, particularly in small towns and rural areas where local businesses serve as economic anchors. For these communities, the tariff mirage had turned into a mirage of stability, a false promise that things would eventually improve once the trade war achieved its goals.

Yet for all the chaos and suffering caused by Trump's tariffs, they remained politically popular, particularly among his base. This was due in part to the way the administration framed the issue. Tariffs were not just economic tools; they were symbols of strength and defiance. Trump repeatedly claimed that the tariffs were forcing China to "pay billions" to the U.S. Treasury, a statement that was both misleading and emblematic of his approach to governance. In reality, the billions collected in tariffs came not from China but from American importers, who then passed the costs onto consumers. This made tariffs a hidden tax on the very people Trump claimed to champion, a financial burden disguised as a patriotic duty.

The leopard, as ever, was feasting. But unlike in the meme, where the victims are caught off guard, Trump's supporters seemed to embrace their role in the spectacle. They believed in the tariffs, not necessarily because they understood the mechanics of international trade, but because they trusted the man selling them. Trump's ability to spin complex issues into simple narratives was one of his greatest political strengths, and tariffs were no exception. He presented them as a way to punish foreign adversaries, protect American jobs, and restore national pride. The fact that they accomplished none of these goals was almost beside the point. What mattered was the story, the feeling of control in a world that often felt uncontrollable.

As the trade war dragged on, however, the cracks in the narrative became harder to ignore. Businesses struggled to adapt to the ever-changing landscape, consumers grew weary of rising prices, and farmers faced an uncertain future in a market that no longer valued their products. The question was no longer whether the tariffs were working, they clearly weren't, but how much longer the administration could maintain the illusion. The tariff mirage, once so bright and enticing, was beginning to fade, revealing the harsh reality of an economy at war with itself.

In the next section of this chapter, we will delve deeper into the long-term consequences of this mirage, from the erosion of America's global standing to the structural damage inflicted on its economy. The leopard may have been invited to the feast, but it was the American people who were left to clean up the mess.

Part 2: The Shattered Mirage

The mirage of tariffs was more than an economic illusion, it was a political sleight of hand, a strategy designed to deflect attention from structural failures by offering the appearance of control. While Part 1 examined how this illusion was crafted and sustained, Part 2 will explore how it fractured under the weight of its contradictions, leaving behind shattered promises, disillusioned voters, and a nation grappling with the consequences of its choices. Tariffs may have been sold as a path to greatness, but they left behind an economy more fragile, fractured, and uncertain than ever.

At the heart of the shattered mirage was the myth that tariffs would bring back American jobs. This promise, central to Trump's rhetoric, resonated deeply with voters in industrial regions who had seen their livelihoods evaporate over decades of deindustrialization. The image of a humming factory floor, staffed by proud workers producing goods stamped with "Made in America," was both powerful and nostalgic. But the reality of the modern economy made such a vision almost impossible to achieve. Automation had replaced millions of manufacturing jobs, and global supply chains had become so entrenched that reversing them would require more than tariffs, it would require a complete overhaul of the economic system, something neither Trump nor his administration had the inclination or expertise to pursue.

The steel and aluminum tariffs of 2018 provided a case study in this failure. While these measures did lead to a modest revival in domestic production, the jobs they created were few and far between, especially when compared to the jobs they destroyed in downstream industries. Automakers, for instance, faced higher costs for raw materials, which squeezed their profit margins and forced them to make cuts elsewhere. Construction companies, already operating on tight budgets, found themselves paying more for steel and aluminum, driving up the cost of projects and delaying investments. The tariffs may have saved a few thousand jobs in the metals industry, but they came at the expense of tens of thousands of jobs elsewhere, a trade-off that left the overall economy worse off.

Even in sectors where jobs did return, the gains were often short-lived. The reopening of steel mills and aluminum plants, heavily touted by the Trump administration, masked deeper vulnerabilities. Many of these facilities relied on government contracts or subsidies to remain viable, and their long-term sustainability was far from guaranteed. Moreover, the jobs themselves often paid less than their predecessors, reflecting the downward pressure on wages that had become a hallmark of the modern economy. For workers who had hoped that tariffs would restore the prosperity of earlier decades, the reality was a bitter pill to swallow.

The agricultural sector, meanwhile, bore the brunt of the retaliatory tariffs imposed by America's trading partners. Farmers, already struggling with declining prices and rising debt, found themselves cut off from key markets as countries like China, Canada, and Mexico imposed steep tariffs on American exports. The $28 billion in bailout payments provided by the Trump administration may have offered temporary relief, but they did little to address the root causes of the crisis. Worse, the payments were distributed unevenly, with large agribusinesses receiving the lion's share while smaller family farms were left to fend for themselves. This deepened the divide between the haves and have-nots in rural America, eroding the sense of community and solidarity that had once been a defining feature of these regions.

For many farmers, the trade war felt like a betrayal. They had supported Trump in 2016, believing his promises to revitalize rural America and protect their way of life. Instead, they found themselves collateral damage in a battle that seemed more about posturing than policy. The relationships they had built with foreign buyers, often over decades, were severed, and rebuilding those connections would take years, if it was even possible. In the meantime, countries like Brazil and Argentina stepped in to fill the void, establishing themselves as reliable suppliers and further diminishing America's share of the global agricultural market.

Retailers and small businesses also found themselves struggling to navigate the new economic landscape. For many of these companies, the rising cost of imported goods was a crushing blow. Retailers, in particular, faced a dilemma: raise prices and risk losing customers, or absorb the costs and risk going out of business. Neither option was sustainable, and the result was a wave of closures and bankruptcies that left communities across the country reeling. Small businesses, often heralded as the backbone of the American economy, were hit particularly hard, as they lacked the resources and flexibility to adapt to the new realities of trade.

The broader economic impact of the tariffs was compounded by the uncertainty they created. Businesses thrive on stability, and

the unpredictability of Trump's trade policies made long-term
planning nearly impossible. Companies that relied on global
supply chains were forced to constantly adjust to new tariffs,
renegotiate contracts, and find alternative suppliers, all of which
added to their costs and reduced their competitiveness. This
uncertainty also discouraged investment, as businesses hesitated
to commit resources to projects that could be upended by the
next round of tariffs. The result was a chilling effect on
economic growth, one that persisted long after the immediate
shock of the tariffs had passed.

On the global stage, America's reputation as a reliable trading
partner took a significant hit. The erratic and often unilateral
nature of Trump's trade policies alienated allies and
emboldened rivals, creating a more fragmented and unstable
international trade system. Countries that had long depended
on America for exports and imports began seeking alternative
partners, wary of the unpredictability that had come to define
the Trump administration. China, in particular, capitalized on
this shift, expanding its influence through initiatives like the Belt
and Road Initiative and strengthening its trade relationships
with other nations. The irony was hard to miss: a trade war
ostensibly designed to counter China's rise had, in many ways,
accelerated it.

The shattered mirage of tariffs also exposed deeper flaws in
America's approach to economic policy. For decades, the
country had relied on the promise of free markets and minimal
government intervention to solve its problems, even as evidence
mounted that this approach was failing large segments of the
population. Tariffs, while ostensibly a departure from this
philosophy, were ultimately just another form of short-term
thinking, a way to paper over deeper issues without addressing
their root causes. The jobs that had been lost to automation,
outsourcing, and globalization weren't coming back, no matter
how high the tariffs. What was needed was a comprehensive
strategy to invest in education, infrastructure, and innovation,
one that prioritized long-term resilience over quick fixes. But

such a strategy required vision, collaboration, and political courage, all qualities that were in short supply.

In the end, the shattered mirage of tariffs left America at a crossroads. The policies had failed to deliver on their promises, but their appeal remained strong, particularly among those who felt abandoned by the existing economic order. The challenge, moving forward, was to offer a credible alternative, one that addressed the real concerns of workers and communities without resorting to the false solutions of the past. Tariffs may have been a seductive mirage, but they were not the answer. The question now was whether America could learn from its mistakes and chart a new course, or whether it would continue to chase illusions, hoping against hope that this time, the leopard wouldn't eat its face.

Part 3: The Lessons of the Leopard

As the dust settled on the trade wars of Trump's first term, it became clear that tariffs were not the solution their proponents had claimed. The leopard had feasted, leaving behind a landscape scarred by higher costs, lost jobs, and fractured relationships both at home and abroad. Yet even as the failures of these policies came into sharper focus, the broader lessons remained elusive. How did we get to a place where the same flawed logic could hold sway, time and again? And more importantly, how could we stop feeding the leopard and start addressing the real issues at the heart of America's economic struggles?

One of the first lessons of the tariff saga is that economic discontent, left unaddressed, is a fertile breeding ground for bad policy. For decades, American workers have been told to trust in the wisdom of free markets and globalization, even as these forces hollowed out entire industries and regions. The rise of the Rust Belt, the collapse of manufacturing towns, and the erosion of stable, well-paying jobs were not accidents; they were the result of deliberate choices made by policymakers who prioritized corporate profits and consumer convenience over the long-term health of communities. When Trump promised to use tariffs to bring back jobs, he was tapping into a wellspring of anger and frustration that had been building for generations. It didn't matter that his solution was flawed; what mattered was that he was offering a solution at all.

This points to a deeper issue: the failure of traditional economic narratives to address the lived experiences of ordinary people. For too long, the benefits of globalization have been framed in abstract terms, **GDP** growth, stock market gains, lower consumer prices, while the costs have been borne by specific communities in very tangible ways. When a factory closes, it's not just jobs that are lost; it's a way of life, a sense of purpose, and the social fabric of an entire region. These losses are hard to quantify, and they rarely make it into the glossy reports of economists or the talking points of politicians. But they are real, and they create a vacuum that populists like Trump are all too eager to fill.

The second lesson is that tariffs, while politically expedient, are fundamentally ill-suited to the challenges of the modern economy. In a globalized world where supply chains span continents and industries are deeply interconnected, the impact of tariffs is never confined to the targeted sector. This was evident in the ripple effects of Trump's steel and aluminum tariffs, which raised costs for downstream industries and dampened economic growth across the board. It was even more apparent in the chaos unleashed by the trade war with China, where businesses, consumers, and farmers all paid the price for policies that failed to achieve their stated goals. Tariffs may have been a useful tool in the 19th century, when economies were more self-contained and trade was less complex. But in the 21st century, they are a blunt instrument, one that often does more harm than good.

Yet for all their flaws, tariffs retain a powerful allure, particularly in times of economic uncertainty. This brings us to the third lesson: the importance of narrative in shaping public perception. Trump's tariffs were not successful by any objective measure, they hurt more than they helped, failed to achieve their goals, and left the economy worse off. But they were framed in a way that made them seem like a victory, at least to those who wanted to believe in them. By portraying tariffs as a way to punish foreign adversaries and protect American jobs, Trump tapped into a deep well of national pride and resentment. The fact that the actual effects of the tariffs contradicted this narrative was almost irrelevant; what mattered was the story being told.

This reliance on narrative over substance is not unique to Trump, nor is it confined to the issue of tariffs. It reflects a broader trend in American politics, where complex issues are often reduced to sound bites and slogans. This simplification may make policies easier to sell, but it also makes them harder to evaluate. When tariffs are framed as a patriotic duty rather than an economic policy, it becomes difficult to have a rational discussion about their merits and drawbacks. The leopard's feast is transformed into a moral imperative, and those who question it are cast as unpatriotic or out of touch.

The fourth lesson is that the costs of bad policy are rarely distributed evenly. While the burden of tariffs fell heavily on workers, consumers, and small businesses, the wealthy and well-connected were largely insulated from their effects. Large corporations with global supply chains were able to adapt by shifting production to non-tariffed countries, passing costs onto customers, or negotiating exemptions. Meanwhile, the small farmers and manufacturers who lacked these resources were left to fend for themselves. This disparity is emblematic of a broader pattern in American economics, where the risks of policy failures are socialized while the rewards are privatized. The leopard eats indiscriminately, but it is always the most vulnerable who suffer the most.

So where do we go from here? The first step is to recognize that tariffs are not a substitute for a coherent economic strategy. If the goal is to create good jobs, reduce inequality, and rebuild communities, there are far better tools available. Investments in education and job training can help workers adapt to the demands of a changing economy. Infrastructure projects can create jobs while laying the foundation for future growth. Tax incentives and grants can encourage innovation and entrepreneurship. And targeted trade agreements can promote fair competition without resorting to the destructive tit-for-tat dynamics of a trade war. These solutions are not as simple or as emotionally satisfying as tariffs, but they have the advantage of actually working.

The second step is to address the underlying causes of economic discontent, rather than simply treating the symptoms. This means acknowledging the failures of globalization and taking steps to mitigate its impact. It means strengthening labor protections, so that workers have a fair share of the wealth they create. It means reforming tax policy to ensure that the benefits of economic growth are more widely shared. And it means investing in the social and economic infrastructure that makes communities resilient, from affordable housing and healthcare to public education and transportation.

Finally, it is crucial to rebuild trust in the institutions that shape economic policy. One of the reasons Trump's tariffs resonated with so many people was that they felt abandoned by the existing system. Decades of broken promises and unfulfilled expectations had eroded their faith in government, business, and even the broader concept of progress. Restoring this trust will require more than just better policies; it will require a commitment to transparency, accountability, and fairness. It will require leaders who are willing to listen, to learn, and to put the needs of the many above the interests of the few.

The leopard's feast is not inevitable. It is the result of choices, choices made by policymakers, by businesses, and by voters. If those choices can be changed, so too can the outcome. But this will require a willingness to look past the mirage, to confront the realities of the modern economy with honesty and courage. It will require a rejection of simplistic solutions and a commitment to addressing the complex, interconnected challenges that define our world. And it will require a recognition that the true strength of a nation lies not in its ability to punish others, but in its capacity to uplift its own people.

In the end, the lesson of the leopard is not just about tariffs or trade wars. It is about the stories we tell ourselves, the choices we make, and the future we are willing to fight for. The leopard may always be hungry, but we don't have to keep feeding it. The power to break the cycle is in our hands, if only we have the courage to use it.

Chapter 3
How Leopards Preyed on the American Dream

Part 1: The Myth of the Self-Made Nation

The idea of America as a self-made nation, forged through grit, determination, and unyielding independence, is one of the most enduring myths in the country's history. It's a story told in countless variations, from Horatio Alger's tales of plucky strivers to modern entrepreneurial icons who claim to have built their empires from nothing. This narrative is seductive because it places the individual at the center of the nation's success, suggesting that anyone with enough drive and ambition can achieve greatness. But like all myths, it is both powerful and deceptive. The reality of America's economic history is far messier, shaped by government intervention, collective effort, and, yes, exploitation. In this chapter, we will unpack the myth of the self-made nation and explore how it has been used to justify policies, like Trump's tariffs, that ultimately serve the interests of the few at the expense of the many.

The self-made myth has always relied on a selective reading of history. It ignores the role of systemic advantages, land grants, subsidies, and other forms of government support, that have underpinned the success of countless "self-made" individuals and industries. Consider the Homestead Act of 1862, which provided free land to settlers willing to farm it. This was a transformative policy, opening vast swaths of the country to development and creating opportunities for millions of Americans. But it also depended on the violent displacement of Indigenous peoples, whose lands were taken without consent. The beneficiaries of the Homestead Act may have worked hard to build their farms, but they did not do so in a vacuum; their success was made possible by government intervention and the exploitation of others.

This pattern repeats throughout American history. The construction of the transcontinental railroad, often hailed as a triumph of private enterprise, was heavily subsidized by federal land grants and loans. The G.I. Bill, which helped create the modern middle class, provided millions of veterans with access to education, housing, and employment opportunities, all funded by the government. Even Silicon Valley, the epitome of self-made entrepreneurial success, owes much of its growth to public investment in technology and infrastructure. None of this is to deny the hard work of individuals, but it is to challenge the notion that success is ever purely a product of individual effort. The self-made myth obscures the role of collective action and public policy in creating the conditions for prosperity.

Trump's tariffs, like so many of his policies, were steeped in the rhetoric of self-reliance. He framed them as a way to restore America's economic independence, to free the nation from its dependence on foreign goods and reclaim its status as a manufacturing powerhouse. This was an appealing narrative, particularly for those who felt left behind by globalization. But it was also a profoundly misleading one. The idea that tariffs could single-handedly restore America's industrial base ignored the structural changes that had reshaped the global economy over the past half-century. Automation, offshoring, and the rise of service industries had fundamentally altered the nature of work, making it impossible to return to the manufacturing-dominated economy of the mid-20th century.

The self-made myth also served to obscure the ways in which tariffs relied on government intervention to achieve their goals. Far from promoting free-market competition, tariffs are a form of economic protectionism, designed to shield domestic industries from foreign competition. This is not inherently a bad thing, many countries use protectionist policies to nurture strategic industries, but it contradicts the idea that success is solely a product of individual or market effort. By imposing tariffs, the government was effectively picking winners and losers, privileging certain industries at the expense of others. Yet this reality was rarely acknowledged in the administration's rhetoric, which continued to tout the tariffs as a testament to America's self-reliance.

Perhaps the most glaring contradiction in the self-made narrative was the way tariffs disproportionately harmed the very people they were supposed to help. Farmers, manufacturers, and small business owners, groups often celebrated as the backbone of the self-made nation, bore the brunt of the economic fallout from Trump's trade policies. Retaliatory tariffs imposed by other countries decimated agricultural exports, while rising costs for imported goods squeezed profit margins and forced difficult choices. These were not the outcomes of a thriving, self-reliant economy; they were the predictable consequences of a policy that ignored the realities of globalization in favor of a nostalgic vision of economic independence.

The harm caused by tariffs was compounded by the uneven distribution of their effects. While the working and middle classes struggled to absorb rising costs, the wealthy and well-connected were largely insulated from the fallout. Large corporations, with their global supply chains and access to capital, were better equipped to adapt to the new trade environment. Some even found ways to profit from the chaos, shifting production to non-tariffed countries or leveraging their political influence to secure exemptions. Meanwhile, small businesses and individual workers were left to bear the costs, further widening the gap between the haves and the have-nots. The self-made myth, far from empowering ordinary Americans, had become a cover for policies that entrenched inequality and concentrated wealth at the top.

This disconnect between rhetoric and reality is not unique to Trump's tariffs. It is a recurring feature of American economic policy, which often pays lip service to the ideals of individualism and self-reliance while implementing policies that serve the interests of the elite. Tax cuts for the wealthy, deregulation of industries, and subsidies for corporations are all framed as measures to promote freedom and opportunity, but their primary effect is to entrench existing power structures. The self-made myth provides a convenient justification for these policies, allowing their proponents to argue that anyone who works hard enough can succeed, even as the deck is stacked against them.

To challenge the self-made myth is not to dismiss the value of hard work or individual initiative. These are important qualities, and they have played a crucial role in America's success. But they are not enough on their own. Prosperity requires more than just effort; it requires opportunity, support, and a level playing field. By focusing exclusively on the individual, the self-made myth ignores the systemic factors that shape economic outcomes and perpetuate inequality. It also creates unrealistic expectations, leading people to blame themselves for failures that are often beyond their control.

As we move into the next section of this chapter, we will delve deeper into the consequences of the self-made myth, exploring how it distorts public policy, perpetuates inequality, and undermines the collective action needed to address the challenges of the modern economy. The leopard, it turns out, is not just an external threat; it is also a reflection of our own beliefs and assumptions. To stop feeding it, we must first confront the myths that sustain it.

Part 2: The False Promises of Individualism

The self-made myth of America, as compelling as it may be, carries with it a darker undertone: the idea that failure is a personal failing, not a systemic one. If the nation is built on the backs of hard-working individuals who supposedly rise through sheer effort, then those who falter or fail must not have worked hard enough. This narrative ignores the structural forces, economic inequality, access to resources, systemic discrimination, that shape individual outcomes. It also creates fertile ground for policies like Trump's tariffs, which lean heavily on the rhetoric of self-reliance while delivering outcomes that deepen systemic inequities. The promises made in the name of individualism are often hollow, serving only to perpetuate the cycle of blame and inaction.

When Trump introduced his tariffs, he framed them as an opportunity for Americans to prove their resilience. The trade war, he argued, was a necessary battle to reclaim American independence and create jobs that would reward hard work and ingenuity. This framing relied on the deeply ingrained belief that the American worker could triumph against any odds, so long as they were given a fair shot. What this narrative failed to acknowledge was that the odds were anything but fair. The global economy is not a level playing field, and decades of policy decisions had systematically disadvantaged certain groups while enriching others. Simply imposing tariffs on foreign goods did nothing to address these underlying imbalances; instead, it exacerbated them.

Take, for example, the agricultural sector, which bore the brunt of retaliatory tariffs from countries like China, Canada, and Mexico. Farmers were told that they just needed to "hold the line," to weather the temporary hardships of the trade war in exchange for long-term gains. But for many, those hardships were anything but temporary. Losing access to major markets like China meant not just a loss of income but the collapse of relationships that had taken years, even decades, to build. Farmers who had invested heavily in equipment, land, and labor based on predictable export demand suddenly found themselves with nowhere to sell their crops. The government bailouts that followed, totaling $28 billion by 2020, were framed as a lifeline, but they were a band-aid at best, doing little to address the long-term damage.

For small family farms, the impact was particularly devastating. These operations, already operating on thin margins, lacked the resources to weather extended periods of uncertainty. Many were forced to sell off land or equipment, taking on crushing debt in an attempt to stay afloat. Meanwhile, larger agribusinesses, which had the capital and political connections to navigate the crisis, often emerged stronger, buying up distressed properties and consolidating their market power. This consolidation further tilted the playing field, making it even harder for smaller farms to compete. The rhetoric of self-reliance, so central to the justification for tariffs, rang hollow in the face of an agricultural sector increasingly dominated by a few powerful players.

The manufacturing sector faced a similar reality. While tariffs were supposed to bring back jobs and revive industrial towns, the actual impact was far more uneven. For every steel mill that reopened, there were dozens of businesses in downstream industries, automotive, construction, appliances, facing higher costs for raw materials. These companies had to make hard choices: raise prices and risk losing customers, absorb the costs and cut into already slim profit margins, or reduce their workforce to stay afloat. In many cases, the latter option prevailed. The tariffs, far from creating jobs, often led to layoffs and closures, particularly in small and medium-sized businesses that lacked the resources to adapt.

Even for the workers who did benefit from the tariffs, the gains were often illusory. Many of the jobs created in the steel and aluminum industries were lower-paying and less secure than the jobs of previous decades. The decline of union power, combined with the rise of contract and gig work, meant that even in industries experiencing growth, workers were left with fewer protections and less bargaining power. The promise of good, stable jobs, jobs that could support a family and build a future, remained out of reach for many. The self-made myth, which glorifies individual effort while ignoring collective action, offered no answers to these systemic challenges.

Perhaps the most insidious consequence of the self-made myth is the way it undermines solidarity. By framing success as a matter of individual effort, it discourages people from working together to address shared challenges. This is particularly evident in the political rhetoric surrounding tariffs, which often pits workers in different industries against each other. Steelworkers are told that their jobs are being sacrificed to benefit consumers who want cheaper goods, while farmers are told that their struggles are the price of protecting manufacturing jobs. This zero-sum framing ignores the reality that all workers are ultimately connected, and that policies designed to divide them serve only to entrench the power of those at the top.

The rhetoric of individualism also obscures the role of government in shaping economic outcomes. When policies like tariffs fail to deliver on their promises, the blame is often placed on individuals, workers for not adapting quickly enough, businesses for not being competitive enough, or consumers for not supporting domestic products. This shifts attention away from the systemic factors that create these challenges in the first place. The uneven distribution of resources, the lack of investment in education and infrastructure, and the dominance of corporate interests in policymaking all play a far greater role in determining economic outcomes than individual effort ever could. Yet these issues are rarely addressed in the debate over tariffs, which remains narrowly focused on questions of fairness and competition.

As the economic consequences of Trump's tariffs became increasingly apparent, the narrative of self-reliance began to show cracks. Farmers, manufacturers, and small business owners who had supported the policy in its early days began to express frustration and disillusionment. They had trusted the promise that hard work and sacrifice would lead to long-term gains, but those gains never materialized. Instead, they were left to pick up the pieces of an economy that seemed more fragile and unequal than ever. For many, this was a bitter lesson in the limits of individualism, a realization that no amount of effort could overcome the structural forces working against them.

Yet even in the face of these failures, the myth of the self-made nation persisted. This is perhaps its greatest strength: its ability to endure, even in the face of overwhelming evidence to the contrary. The promise of individualism is deeply ingrained in the American psyche, a source of both inspiration and delusion. It allows people to believe in the possibility of upward mobility, even as the barriers to that mobility grow ever higher. It offers hope in times of uncertainty, even as it blinds people to the need for collective action. And it provides a convenient scapegoat for systemic failures, allowing policymakers to avoid accountability and shift the burden onto those who can least afford it.

As we move into the final section of this chapter, we will explore the long-term consequences of the self-made myth, both for America's economy and its political culture. We will also consider the possibilities for a new narrative, one that emphasizes cooperation over competition and recognizes the value of shared responsibility. The false promises of individualism may have brought us to this point, but they do not have to define our future.

Part 3: Toward a Collective Reality

The myth of the self-made nation, as seductive as it is, has always been inadequate for addressing the complexities of a modern, interconnected world. In its celebration of individual grit and perseverance, it neglects the systemic realities that define economic success or failure. It leaves little room for acknowledging the role of community, government, and shared responsibility in shaping outcomes. Trump's tariffs, steeped in the language of self-reliance, epitomized the dangers of this myth. Their failures not only exposed the hollowness of promises tied to the self-made ideal but also provided a stark reminder of the urgent need for a more collective understanding of economic policy. This final section examines how America might move beyond the self-made myth toward a narrative that recognizes the interconnectedness of its citizens and the importance of shared effort.

The tariff policies of Trump's presidency were a reflection of the self-made myth's most damaging tendencies. By framing tariffs as a tool to restore American greatness, the administration effectively placed the burden of economic recovery on the shoulders of individuals. Workers were told that the tariffs would bring back their jobs, as if the forces that had displaced those jobs, automation, globalization, and corporate greed, could be undone with a single policy. Farmers were asked to endure the pain of retaliatory tariffs, with the promise that their sacrifices would ultimately lead to greater prosperity. Consumers, meanwhile, were expected to shoulder rising prices as a patriotic duty, a small price to pay for the supposed benefits of economic independence. In every case, the underlying assumption was that individuals, not systems, were responsible for making the policy work.

But the failures of the tariffs revealed a deeper truth: no amount of individual effort can compensate for systemic dysfunction. Farmers who lost access to international markets could not simply work harder to replace those lost revenues. Manufacturers facing higher input costs could not innovate their way out of the economic constraints created by the trade war. Workers who lost their jobs because their employers could no longer compete in a tariff-distorted market were not to blame for their misfortune. These were not failures of effort or ingenuity; they were failures of policy, born out of a refusal to confront the realities of a globalized economy.

The self-made myth, for all its flaws, persists because it offers a comforting sense of agency. It tells people that their success or failure is within their control, that they are the masters of their own destiny. But this illusion comes at a cost. By placing the burden of success solely on the individual, it obscures the systemic barriers that prevent many from achieving their potential. It also discourages collective action, fostering a sense of competition rather than collaboration. If everyone is supposed to fend for themselves, the idea of working together to address shared challenges becomes not just unnecessary but counterproductive.

Trump's tariffs were emblematic of this mindset, prioritizing short-term, individualistic gains over long-term, collective solutions. Instead of addressing the root causes of economic insecurity, rising inequality, declining union power, and the lack of investment in education and infrastructure, the administration pursued a policy that pitted industries and workers against each other. Steelworkers were promised that tariffs would protect their jobs, even as downstream industries faced layoffs and closures. Farmers were told to hold the line, even as agribusinesses consolidated power at their expense. The result was not a stronger economy but a more divided one, where the costs of bad policy were borne disproportionately by those least able to afford them.

If America is to move beyond the failures of the self-made myth, it must first acknowledge the interconnectedness of its economy and society. The challenges facing the nation, whether they are economic, social, or environmental, cannot be solved by individuals acting alone. They require collective action, supported by policies that recognize the value of cooperation and shared responsibility. This means rejecting the zero-sum thinking that has long dominated American politics, where the success of one group is seen as coming at the expense of another. Instead, the focus must shift to creating a system where prosperity is broadly shared and where the success of one sector or community contributes to the well-being of the whole.

One way to achieve this is by reframing the role of government in the economy. For too long, government intervention has been portrayed as antithetical to the ideals of the self-made nation, a hindrance rather than a help. But history tells a different story. From the New Deal to the G.I. Bill to the infrastructure investments of the postwar era, government policies have played a crucial role in creating opportunities for individuals and communities to thrive. Recognizing this role does not mean abandoning the values of hard work and individual initiative; it means acknowledging that these values are most effective when supported by a foundation of shared resources and collective effort.

A collective approach to economic policy would also require rethinking the nation's relationship with globalization. The idea that America can, or should, stand alone in the global economy is not just unrealistic but counterproductive. Trade is not inherently harmful; it is a source of innovation, growth, and connection. The challenge is not to reject globalization outright but to ensure that its benefits are distributed more equitably. This could mean negotiating trade agreements that prioritize labor rights and environmental protections, investing in industries that create good jobs at home, and providing support for workers and communities affected by economic transitions.

Another crucial element of a collective approach is addressing the structural inequalities that have been exacerbated by policies like tariffs. This means strengthening labor protections, so that workers have a fair share of the wealth they create. It means reforming the tax system to ensure that the wealthy and corporations pay their fair share, funding investments in education, healthcare, and infrastructure. It also means recognizing and addressing the ways in which systemic discrimination, whether based on race, gender, or geography, limits opportunities for many Americans. These are not issues that can be solved by individual effort alone; they require a concerted, collective response.

Finally, moving beyond the self-made myth would require a shift in cultural values. The idea of rugged individualism is deeply ingrained in the American psyche, but it is not the only way to define success. Other cultures emphasize the importance of community, collaboration, and mutual support, values that are equally compatible with the ideals of freedom and opportunity. By embracing these values, America could build a more inclusive and resilient economy, one that recognizes the contributions of all its citizens and ensures that no one is left behind.

The failures of Trump's tariffs were not just economic; they were symbolic of a broader failure to confront the limitations of the self-made myth. By clinging to a narrative that prioritizes individual effort over systemic solutions, the nation has limited its ability to address the challenges of the modern world. But these failures also offer an opportunity. They provide a chance to reimagine what it means to be a self-reliant nation, not as a collection of individuals competing for scarce resources, but as a community working together to create shared prosperity. The leopard may always be hungry, but it doesn't have to be fed. By confronting the myths that sustain it, America can build a future where everyone has the opportunity to thrive, not alone, but together.

Note: Tariffs and Labor Protections

Tariffs are closely linked to the erosion of labor protections and the decline of economic mobility, highlighting their limitations as tools for supporting workers in the modern economy. Historically, strong labor protections, such as collective bargaining and fair wage laws, ensured that economic policies like tariffs benefited workers rather than just corporations. Over the past century, however, the decline of unions, the rise of gig and precarious work, and stagnating wages have weakened workers' ability to share in economic gains. When Trump implemented tariffs on steel, aluminum, and Chinese goods, the promise was to bring back jobs and revitalize American industry. In reality, the benefits primarily flowed to corporate executives and shareholders, while workers experienced stagnant wages, limited job security, and rising costs. Tariffs without strong labor protections left industries under no obligation to improve working conditions or pay, failing to deliver on their promises.

Moreover, the ripple effects of tariffs in downstream industries like automotive manufacturing and construction further undermined their supposed benefits. By raising input costs for these sectors, tariffs forced businesses, already weakened by declining labor protections and shrinking profit margins, to make cuts. Many responded by reducing jobs, hours, or pay, while others passed costs onto consumers, increasing financial pressures on households. Workers in low-wage and precarious positions, who already lacked access to traditional protections like collective bargaining, were hit hardest by rising prices for goods and the economic uncertainty tariffs created. This highlighted the gap between rhetoric and reality: while tariffs were framed as tools to protect workers, they often exacerbated the challenges faced by the most vulnerable, including reduced economic mobility and growing income inequality.

Ultimately, tariffs fail to address the structural forces driving economic insecurity, such as globalization, automation, and the decline of worker power. Without strong protections like unionization, fair wages, and investments in worker retraining, tariffs are incapable of reversing decades of disinvestment in the workforce. They offer temporary relief to a few industries while failing to create pathways for long-term worker prosperity. Meanwhile, the lack of robust safety nets leaves those affected by trade disruptions or rising costs with few options, further entrenching inequality. Tariffs, when used without systemic reforms to labor protections, become tools that widen the gap between executives and workers rather than bridging it. This underscores the urgent need to prioritize policies that strengthen worker power, promote fair wages, and create shared prosperity, elements that tariffs alone cannot deliver.

54

Chapter 4
Leopard Economics — The Cost of Lies

Part 1: The Cost of False Promises

The allure of false promises in economic policy is as old as
politics itself, and tariffs are one of the most enduring examples.
They represent a potent mix of hope and hubris, offering simple
answers to complex problems while masking the true costs that
lie beneath the surface. Throughout history, tariffs have been
wielded not only as tools of economic policy but also as symbols
of national pride and defiance. In Trump's hands, tariffs
became both a political weapon and a rhetorical flourish, a way
to tap into deep-seated grievances about globalization, job
losses, and perceived unfairness in international trade. Yet, as
with so many policies sold on the basis of symbolism rather than
substance, the promises made to the American people were
never fully delivered. Instead, the costs, economic, social, and
political, accumulated quietly, falling disproportionately on the
shoulders of those least equipped to bear them.

At the heart of Trump's tariff policy was the promise of
economic revival, a pledge to bring back the manufacturing jobs
that had been lost to globalization and technological change. It
was a compelling vision, one that resonated deeply in
communities that had seen factories shuttered and livelihoods
disappear. For many, tariffs were not just a policy but a lifeline,
a chance to restore dignity and purpose in places that had been
written off as casualties of the modern economy. Yet this vision
was built on a foundation of misconceptions about the nature of
economic change and the forces driving job losses.
Globalization and free trade agreements were often blamed for
the decline of American manufacturing, but the reality was far
more complex. Automation, corporate consolidation, and
decades of disinvestment in worker training and education
played equally significant roles in reshaping the labor market.

Tariffs, no matter how sweeping or aggressive, could do little to address these deeper structural issues.

The steel and aluminum tariffs of 2018 exemplified the limitations of this approach. Initially framed as a way to protect national security and revitalize domestic production, these tariffs did succeed in boosting output in a handful of facilities. Steel mills reopened, and a few thousand jobs were added to the sector, prompting Trump to claim victory. But these gains were short-lived and came at a steep price. Industries reliant on steel and aluminum, automotive, construction, and aerospace, to name a few, faced skyrocketing input costs, forcing them to make difficult choices. Some cut back on hiring, others delayed projects, and many passed the increased costs onto consumers. For every job saved or created in the steel industry, several were lost downstream, a trade-off that was largely ignored in the administration's celebratory rhetoric.

This pattern repeated itself across the broader trade war with China, where the costs of tariffs were felt most acutely by farmers, small businesses, and low-income households. Farmers, in particular, found themselves on the front lines of the economic conflict, as China responded to U.S. tariffs with retaliatory measures targeting agricultural exports. Soybean farmers, who had long relied on China as their largest market, saw demand evaporate almost overnight, leaving them with unsold crops and mounting debt. The federal government's bailout programs, totaling $28 billion by the end of 2020, provided some relief but failed to address the root causes of the crisis. Many farmers were forced to sell their land or take on additional loans, and the long-term damage to U.S. agricultural exports was profound. China, unwilling to remain dependent on an unpredictable trading partner, turned to other suppliers, establishing new relationships that would be difficult to dislodge even after the trade war subsided.

For small businesses, the impact of tariffs was equally devastating. Lacking the resources and flexibility of larger corporations, many were unable to adapt to the rising costs of imported goods. Retailers, in particular, struggled to maintain profitability as prices for everything from electronics to clothing increased. Some absorbed the costs, cutting into already narrow profit margins, while others raised prices and risked alienating customers. For many, the combination of higher costs and reduced demand proved insurmountable, leading to closures and layoffs that further destabilized local economies. These were not just economic losses but social ones, as small businesses often serve as anchors for their communities, providing not only jobs but also a sense of identity and connection.

Even consumers, the supposed beneficiaries of tariffs, found themselves worse off. Despite promises that tariffs would protect American workers and lower unemployment, the reality was that most households faced higher prices for everyday goods. From groceries to household appliances, the cost of living increased, putting additional strain on family budgets already stretched thin by stagnant wages and rising healthcare expenses. Low-income households were hit hardest, as they spend a larger proportion of their income on necessities and are less able to absorb price increases. The very people who were meant to benefit from Trump's tariff policies were often the ones who suffered the most, caught in a cycle of higher costs and limited economic opportunity.

The broader economic impact of tariffs was compounded by their effect on business investment and innovation. In an environment of constant uncertainty, where tariffs could be announced, increased, or rescinded with little warning, many companies chose to delay or scale back investments in new projects. This chilling effect on capital expenditure slowed economic growth and reduced opportunities for job creation, undermining the very goals tariffs were supposed to achieve. For industries dependent on global supply chains, the unpredictability of trade policy made long-term planning nearly impossible, forcing businesses to focus on short-term survival rather than innovation and expansion. This was particularly damaging in high-tech sectors, where the ability to compete globally depends on continuous investment in research and development.

Internationally, the costs of Trump's tariffs extended beyond economics to diplomacy and global trade relations. By pursuing a unilateral approach to trade policy, the administration alienated key allies and undermined multilateral institutions like the World Trade Organization (WTO). Countries that had traditionally relied on the United States as a trading partner began seeking alternatives, forging new alliances and trade agreements that excluded American interests. China, in particular, capitalized on the disruption, expanding its influence through initiatives like the Belt and Road Initiative and deepening its relationships with other trading partners. Far from weakening China's position, the trade war often strengthened it, as Beijing used the opportunity to solidify its role as a global economic leader.

These international dynamics highlighted a fundamental flaw in the administration's approach: the failure to recognize the interconnectedness of the global economy. Tariffs, by their very nature, disrupt these connections, creating inefficiencies and imbalances that ripple across borders. In a world where supply chains span continents and markets are deeply intertwined, the idea that any country can act in isolation is a dangerous illusion. The costs of this illusion were felt not only by American businesses and consumers but also by the broader global economy, which faced increased uncertainty and slower growth as a result of the trade war.

As the economic and political costs of tariffs mounted, the question of accountability became increasingly important. Who bore the responsibility for these failures? Was it the policymakers who had crafted and implemented the tariffs, or the voters who had supported them? The answer, of course, is both. Tariffs were not imposed in a vacuum; they were the product of a political system that rewards short-term thinking

and symbolic gestures over substantive solutions. They were also
the result of a deeply ingrained narrative about American
exceptionalism and self-reliance, a narrative that often blinds
people to the realities of a globalized world.

In the next part of this chapter, we will delve deeper into the
political and cultural forces that sustain this narrative, exploring
how the myth of the self-made nation continues to shape policy
and public perception. We will also consider the lessons to be
learned from the failures of Trump's tariff policies, and the steps
that could be taken to build a more equitable and resilient
economy. The cost of false promises is not just economic; it is
also social, cultural, and moral. Understanding these costs is the
first step toward creating a future where policy is guided by
reality rather than rhetoric.

Part 2: The Political Mythmaking (Lies) of Tariffs

The story of tariffs, as told by politicians and policymakers, is
less about economics and more about mythmaking. Over
generations, tariffs have been cast as instruments of national
pride and economic justice, tools that safeguard the
hardworking American against foreign threats and greedy
competitors. These narratives resonate because they simplify
complex global realities into a battle between "us" and "them,"
playing on fears, anxieties, and the longing for a return to an
imagined golden age of prosperity. In Trump's presidency, this
myth reached its most visible and aggressive form, wielded as a
rallying cry for a nation struggling to reconcile its ideals of self-
reliance with the realities of a globalized economy. But as the
costs of his policies mounted, it became clear that the myth was
a double-edged sword, powerful in its appeal, yet destructive in
its consequences.

To understand the political utility of tariffs, it is important to
recognize their symbolic power. Tariffs are not merely taxes on
imports; they are declarations of intent. A tariff signals that the

government is taking action, that it is willing to stand up for domestic industries and workers against foreign competition. This symbolism is especially potent in times of economic uncertainty, when people are looking for tangible evidence that their leaders are fighting for them. Trump capitalized on this dynamic, framing his tariffs as bold measures to protect American jobs and restore the nation's manufacturing prowess. In his speeches and tweets, he portrayed himself as a warrior battling unfair trade practices, using tariffs as his weapon of choice. The simplicity of this narrative made it compelling, even as its flaws became increasingly apparent.

The power of the tariff myth lies in its ability to create a clear villain. In Trump's rhetoric, this villain was China, portrayed as a manipulative and exploitative power that had taken advantage of America's generosity for decades. By imposing tariffs on Chinese goods, Trump claimed to be leveling the playing field, forcing Beijing to play fair. This framing resonated with many Americans who felt that globalization had left them behind, giving them a target for their frustrations. The narrative also tapped into deeper fears about China's growing influence, turning the trade war into a broader cultural and geopolitical conflict. But while this narrative may have been effective politically, it was disconnected from the economic realities of the global supply chain, where goods often pass through multiple countries before reaching consumers. Tariffs on Chinese goods often ended up punishing American businesses and consumers just as much, if not more, than their intended target.

One of the great ironies of Trump's tariff policies was how they revealed the fragility of the industries they were supposed to protect. For decades, American manufacturing had been hollowed out by a combination of automation, offshoring, and corporate consolidation. Many of the factories that had closed were not victims of unfair trade practices but of technological advancements and market shifts that made certain jobs obsolete. Tariffs could not turn back the clock on these changes, but the myth suggested otherwise. By promising to bring back jobs,

Trump offered a vision of economic revival that ignored the structural realities of the modern economy. This disconnect between rhetoric and reality became increasingly evident as the costs of the trade war mounted.

Farmers, who were among Trump's most loyal supporters, bore some of the heaviest burdens of the trade war. China's retaliatory tariffs on American agricultural products devastated rural communities, cutting off access to key markets and driving down prices for crops and livestock. For many farmers, the promise of tariffs as a tool to protect American interests turned into a bitter joke. Federal bailout programs provided some relief, but they were poorly targeted, with large agribusinesses often receiving the lion's share of the benefits. Meanwhile, small family farms struggled to survive, taking on debt or selling off land to make ends meet. The myth of the self-made farmer, working hard and reaping the rewards of their labor, was undermined by the stark reality of government dependency and economic precarity.

The broader economic effects of tariffs also highlighted the limitations of the myth. By raising the cost of imported goods, tariffs acted as a hidden tax on consumers, disproportionately affecting low- and middle-income households. Families already struggling with stagnant wages and rising living costs found themselves paying more for essentials like clothing, electronics, and appliances. This was not the economic revival that had been promised; it was a redistribution of costs from one group to another, with little to show for it in terms of long-term benefits. The political appeal of tariffs as a tool to protect workers and industries was undermined by the reality that they often caused more harm than good.

Yet for all their failures, the narrative surrounding tariffs remained resilient. This was in part because the myth of protectionism is deeply ingrained in American political culture. From the earliest days of the republic, tariffs have been used as a tool to promote domestic industry and assert national sovereignty. In the 19th century, they played a key role in funding the government and protecting emerging industries from foreign competition. Even as the economy evolved, the symbolic power of tariffs persisted, tied to broader themes of independence, fairness, and self-reliance. Trump's use of tariffs was a continuation of this tradition, albeit in a form that prioritized short-term political gains over long-term economic strategy.

Another reason for the resilience of the tariff myth is its emotional appeal. Tariffs tap into a sense of nostalgia, a longing for a time when America was seen as the unchallenged leader of the global economy. They offer the promise of control in a world that feels increasingly chaotic and interconnected, a way to reclaim sovereignty and protect national interests. This emotional resonance makes it difficult to challenge the narrative, even when the evidence contradicts it. For many people, the idea of tariffs as a tool of economic justice is too compelling to abandon, regardless of their actual impact.

The political utility of tariffs also lies in their ability to shift blame. By framing economic challenges as the result of unfair trade practices by foreign countries, politicians can deflect attention from domestic policy failures. This was a key feature of Trump's rhetoric, which often focused on the actions of China, Mexico, or the European Union while ignoring the role of American corporations and policymakers in driving inequality and economic insecurity. By presenting tariffs as a way to hold others accountable, the administration avoided confronting the deeper systemic issues that required attention, such as wage stagnation, declining union power, and the lack of investment in education and infrastructure.

As the trade war dragged on, the costs of this political mythmaking became increasingly clear. Businesses, consumers, and workers all faced rising uncertainty and economic hardship, while the promised benefits of tariffs failed to materialize. The broader global economy also suffered, with disruptions to supply chains and trade flows creating inefficiencies and slowing growth. Yet the narrative persisted, fueled by the same fears and frustrations that had made it so effective in the first place. The question, then, is not just why the myth of tariffs endures, but what it would take to replace it with a narrative that better reflects the realities of the modern economy.

In the next section of this chapter, we will explore the consequences of this mythmaking in greater detail, examining how it distorts public policy and undermines efforts to address the root causes of economic insecurity. We will also consider the potential for alternative narratives that emphasize cooperation, shared responsibility, and the interconnectedness of global markets. The cost of false promises, as we will see, extends far beyond economics, shaping the political and cultural landscape in ways that are difficult to reverse.

Part 3: The Long Shadow of Tariff Politics

The long-term effects of tariffs extend far beyond their immediate economic consequences, leaving a deep and often invisible imprint on public policy, political culture, and societal attitudes. When tariffs are used not as nuanced tools of economic strategy but as blunt instruments of political theater, their legacy becomes one of division, mistrust, and wasted opportunities. Trump's tariff policies, built on a foundation of populist rhetoric and economic simplifications, exemplified this trend. They were sold as a path to renewal and independence but instead entrenched the very inequalities and inefficiencies they claimed to combat. The question is not merely how tariffs failed but why they were allowed to fail so spectacularly and what this failure reveals about the broader political and cultural dynamics of modern America.

One of the most significant and enduring legacies of Trump's tariffs is the erosion of trust in government and economic policy. For many Americans, the promise of tariffs was not just about

jobs or trade; it was about a broader sense of fairness and
justice. Tariffs were framed as a way to correct systemic
imbalances, to punish those who had taken advantage of
America's goodwill, and to restore opportunities for ordinary
workers. When these promises went unfulfilled, when jobs failed
to return, prices rose, and businesses struggled, many people
were left feeling betrayed. This sense of disillusionment was
particularly acute in rural and industrial communities that had
placed their faith in Trump's rhetoric, believing that he would
deliver the revival they had long been waiting for.

This erosion of trust is not unique to tariffs but is symptomatic
of a broader pattern in American politics, where symbolic
policies are often used to paper over systemic problems without
addressing their root causes. By focusing on tariffs as a solution
to the challenges of globalization and economic insecurity, the
Trump administration avoided tackling the deeper issues of
wage stagnation, declining union power, and the lack of
investment in education and infrastructure. This strategy, while
politically expedient, left many of the underlying problems
unaddressed, creating a cycle of disillusionment and frustration
that has become a defining feature of American public life. The
failure of tariffs thus became part of a larger narrative of
institutional failure, reinforcing the belief that government
cannot or will not act in the interests of ordinary people.

Another lasting consequence of the tariff policies was the
deepening of economic inequalities. While tariffs were ostensibly
designed to protect American workers, their actual effects often
benefited the wealthy and well-connected at the expense of
everyone else. Large corporations, with their global supply
chains and access to capital, were able to adapt to the new trade
environment, often by shifting production to non-tariffed
countries or negotiating exemptions. Small businesses and
workers, on the other hand, lacked these resources and were left
to bear the brunt of the disruptions caused by tariffs. This
uneven distribution of costs and benefits further widened the

gap between the haves and the have-nots, exacerbating the very inequalities that tariffs were supposed to address.

The political discourse surrounding tariffs also contributed to a broader culture of division and scapegoating. By framing trade imbalances as the result of unfair practices by foreign countries, the Trump administration created an "us versus them" narrative that oversimplified complex global dynamics and pitted Americans against perceived external enemies. This rhetoric was effective in rallying political support but had the unintended consequence of fostering mistrust and animosity, both domestically and internationally. At home, it deepened divisions between workers in different industries, as some were seen as beneficiaries of tariffs while others bore their costs. Abroad, it strained relationships with key allies and trading partners, undermining the cooperation needed to address shared challenges in a globalized world.

Perhaps the most profound impact of Trump's tariffs was their role in perpetuating the myth of economic independence. The idea that America can isolate itself from the global economy and thrive on its own terms is a seductive one, but it is increasingly at odds with reality. Modern supply chains are deeply interconnected, and the prosperity of one nation is often tied to the prosperity of others. Tariffs, by disrupting these connections, create inefficiencies that ultimately hurt everyone involved. Yet the myth persists, fueled by a combination of nostalgia, fear, and political opportunism. By doubling down on this narrative, the Trump administration not only failed to prepare Americans for the realities of a globalized economy but also left the country less competitive and less resilient in the face of future challenges.

The cultural impact of tariffs is equally significant, shaping attitudes toward work, trade, and the role of government. By framing tariffs as a way to protect the American worker, the administration reinforced the idea that economic success is a zero-sum game, where the gains of one group come at the expense of another. This perspective, while politically expedient, ignores the potential for cooperation and shared prosperity. It also perpetuates a sense of scarcity and competition that undermines solidarity and collective action. In a society where workers are pitted against one another and against the rest of the world, it becomes difficult to build the trust and collaboration needed to address systemic issues like inequality and climate change.

The long shadow of tariff politics also extends to America's role on the global stage. By pursuing a unilateral and confrontational approach to trade policy, the Trump administration weakened the institutions and alliances that have underpinned the global economy for decades. The erosion of trust in multilateral organizations like the World Trade Organization (WTO) and the alienation of key allies created a more fragmented and unstable trade environment, with ripple effects that are still being felt today. This shift has not only harmed America's economic interests but also its geopolitical standing, as countries like China have stepped into the void, expanding their influence and consolidating their power.

As the dust settles on Trump's tariff policies, the question remains: what lessons can be learned from their failures, and how can these lessons inform future policymaking? The first and most obvious lesson is that tariffs are not a panacea. While they can be effective in specific contexts, such as protecting nascent industries or addressing unfair trade practices, they are not a substitute for a comprehensive economic strategy. Addressing the challenges of globalization and economic insecurity requires a multifaceted approach, one that includes investments in education, infrastructure, and worker training, as well as policies to strengthen labor protections and reduce income inequality.

The second lesson is the importance of transparency and accountability in policymaking. One of the key flaws of Trump's tariff policies was the lack of a clear and coherent strategy. Tariffs were announced and implemented with little warning, creating uncertainty and confusion for businesses and consumers alike. Moving forward, policymakers must prioritize clear communication and evidence-based decision-making, ensuring that economic policies are designed to achieve specific, measurable goals rather than serving as tools of political theater.

Finally, the failure of tariffs underscores the need for a new narrative about America's place in the global economy. The myth of economic independence is not only outdated but harmful, preventing the country from engaging constructively with the rest of the world. A more realistic and forward-looking narrative would emphasize the benefits of cooperation and interconnectedness, recognizing that America's prosperity is tied to the prosperity of others. This narrative would also highlight the importance of shared responsibility, challenging the individualistic ethos that has long dominated American political culture.

In the end, the long shadow of tariff politics is a reminder of the dangers of prioritizing symbolism over substance. The costs of false promises are not just economic but also social and political, shaping attitudes and institutions in ways that are difficult to undo. Yet within these failures lies an opportunity: the chance to learn from the past and chart a new course, one that prioritizes equity, resilience, and shared prosperity over divisive rhetoric and short-term gains. The challenge is immense, but the stakes are too high to ignore. Only by confronting the myths that have held us back can we begin to build a future that works for everyone.

Chapter 5
The Leopard's Bite – Your $4,000 Price Tage

Part 1: The Illusion of Economic Strength

Economic strength has long been a cornerstone of national identity and political power in the United States. From the post-World War II industrial boom to the tech-driven prosperity of the 21st century, America has built its image as the world's economic leader on the foundation of innovation, production, and consumption. Yet, the narrative of economic strength often obscures deeper vulnerabilities. Beneath the surface lies an economy marked by inequality, fragility, and systemic inefficiencies, where short-term gains are frequently prioritized over long-term resilience. The Trump administration's tariff policies fit neatly into this pattern, presenting the illusion of strength while exacerbating the structural weaknesses they purported to address.

The appeal of tariffs as a symbol of economic strength is easy to understand. They are tangible, measurable, and easily framed as a form of self-defense in a competitive global market. In speeches and rallies, Trump often invoked the imagery of battle, casting America as a nation under siege by unfair trade practices and tariffs as the weapons needed to fight back. This framing was particularly effective in manufacturing regions, where the decline of traditional industries had left communities feeling abandoned and disempowered. Tariffs were sold as a way to reclaim lost ground, to restore the jobs and prosperity that globalization and automation had taken away. For many, this message offered a sense of agency and hope, a belief that the government was finally standing up for their interests.

But the reality of tariffs, as always, was far more complex. While they can provide temporary protection for specific industries, their broader economic impact is often counterproductive. By raising the cost of imports, tariffs disrupt supply chains, increase prices for consumers, and create inefficiencies that ripple through the economy. For businesses reliant on foreign materials or components, tariffs force difficult choices: absorb the additional costs, raise prices, or cut back on operations. These decisions, in turn, affect workers and consumers, often undermining the very economic strength tariffs are meant to bolster.

The steel and aluminum tariffs of 2018 provide a clear example of this dynamic. Initially framed as a national security measure, these tariffs were intended to protect domestic metal producers and reduce dependence on foreign suppliers. In the short term, they did achieve some of their goals, leading to increased production and job growth in the steel and aluminum industries. Trump frequently touted these successes, pointing to reopened mills and new hires as evidence that his policies were working. However, these gains came at a significant cost to downstream industries like automotive manufacturing, construction, and appliances, which rely heavily on affordable steel and aluminum. Higher input costs forced many of these companies to raise prices, cut jobs, or delay investments, creating a ripple effect that offset the benefits of the tariffs.

This pattern of short-term gains and long-term costs was repeated throughout the trade war with China. The administration's tariffs on Chinese goods, which targeted everything from electronics to textiles, were intended to address a wide range of grievances, including intellectual property theft, forced technology transfers, and trade imbalances. Yet, rather than forcing China to capitulate, the tariffs led to a tit-for-tat escalation, with Beijing imposing its own tariffs on American exports. The resulting uncertainty disrupted global supply chains and created economic hardship for businesses and consumers on both sides. In the United States, the costs of the trade war were felt most acutely by farmers, who lost access to key export markets, and by low-income households, who faced rising prices for everyday goods.

One of the most striking aspects of Trump's tariff policies was their reliance on the illusion of strength rather than actual results. While the administration frequently highlighted isolated successes, such as the revival of specific factories or the renegotiation of trade agreements, these achievements were often overshadowed by broader economic losses. For every job saved in the steel industry, for example, several were lost in downstream industries. For every deal struck with a trading partner, new barriers were erected elsewhere. Yet, the narrative of strength persisted, bolstered by the administration's ability to control the messaging around its policies. This disconnect between rhetoric and reality is a hallmark of policies designed more for political theater than for economic substance.

The illusion of economic strength created by tariffs was not limited to their direct effects. It also shaped public perceptions of broader economic trends, reinforcing a narrative of resilience and independence that masked deeper vulnerabilities. By framing tariffs as a way to reduce dependence on foreign suppliers, the administration tapped into a long-standing belief in the virtues of self-reliance and national sovereignty. This narrative, while emotionally compelling, ignored the realities of the modern global economy, where supply chains are deeply interconnected and no country can truly stand alone. The disruption caused by tariffs often highlighted these interdependencies, as businesses struggled to adapt to sudden changes in trade policy. Yet, rather than acknowledging these challenges, the administration doubled down on the rhetoric of strength, insisting that short-term pain was necessary for long-term gain.

The costs of maintaining this illusion were not merely economic but also political and social. By framing tariffs as a solution to complex problems like globalization and income inequality, the administration deflected attention from the deeper systemic issues that required action. The challenges facing American workers, stagnant wages, declining union power, and rising healthcare costs, could not be solved by tariffs alone, yet these issues were often sidelined in the broader conversation about trade. This focus on symbolic policies over substantive reforms left many workers feeling disillusioned and betrayed when the promised benefits of tariffs failed to materialize.

Moreover, the reliance on tariffs as a symbol of strength contributed to a broader culture of division and scapegoating. By casting foreign countries as villains in the story of America's economic struggles, the administration reinforced a narrative of competition and conflict that undermined the potential for cooperation and shared prosperity. This approach not only strained relationships with key trading partners but also deepened domestic divisions, as workers in different industries were pitted against one another. Steelworkers, for example, were seen as beneficiaries of tariffs, while farmers and consumers bore the costs. This zero-sum framing made it difficult to build the solidarity needed to address shared challenges, further weakening the foundation of America's economic strength.

In the next section of this chapter, we will explore the broader implications of this illusion, examining how the reliance on tariffs and other symbolic policies distorts public policy and undermines the pursuit of long-term economic resilience. We will also consider the steps that could be taken to move beyond this pattern, focusing on strategies that prioritize equity, sustainability, and shared prosperity over short-term political gains. The illusion of economic strength, as compelling as it may be, is ultimately a fragile foundation for a nation's future. Recognizing its limitations is the first step toward building a more resilient and inclusive economy.

Part 2: The Ripple Effect of Symbolic Policies

While tariffs under Trump's administration were marketed as bold steps toward economic resurgence, their effects rippled far beyond their immediate targets, creating unintended consequences for industries, workers, and communities. This ripple effect revealed the true nature of symbolic policies: their capacity to generate more disruption than progress. While the administration heralded tariffs as a show of strength, the reality was that these measures exacerbated existing economic vulnerabilities, sowed uncertainty, and distracted from addressing systemic challenges. As the impacts unfolded, it became increasingly clear that the symbolism of tariffs carried far more weight than their substance.

At the core of this ripple effect was the interconnectedness of the modern economy. Supply chains, once localized, now span continents, linking manufacturers, suppliers, and consumers in a delicate web of interdependence. Tariffs, by their nature, disrupt these connections, creating inefficiencies and bottlenecks that reverberate throughout the system. Take, for instance, the automotive industry, which relies heavily on imported components such as steel and aluminum. When Trump imposed tariffs on these metals, the immediate result was an increase in production costs for automakers. These costs were either passed on to consumers in the form of higher prices or absorbed by companies, reducing their profit margins and limiting their ability to invest in innovation and growth. Neither outcome advanced the administration's stated goal of strengthening American manufacturing.

For smaller businesses, the ripple effects were even more pronounced. Unlike multinational corporations, which have the resources and flexibility to adapt to changing trade policies, small and medium-sized enterprises (SMEs) often operate on razor-thin margins and lack the capacity to reconfigure supply chains on short notice. When faced with rising costs due to tariffs, many SMEs were forced to make painful decisions: reduce their workforce, scale back production, or even shutter their operations entirely. These closures were not just economic losses; they were also social ones, as small businesses often serve as anchors for their communities, providing jobs, services, and a sense of identity.

The agricultural sector, long a symbol of American self-reliance, was among the hardest hit by the trade war's ripple effects.

When China imposed retaliatory tariffs on U.S. soybeans, pork, and other agricultural products, the impact on American farmers was immediate and devastating. Markets that had taken years to cultivate were suddenly closed off, leaving farmers with surplus crops and plummeting prices. While the federal government attempted to mitigate these losses with bailout programs totaling $28 billion, the aid was unevenly distributed and often came too late to save smaller farms from bankruptcy. Meanwhile, countries like Brazil and Argentina capitalized on the opportunity to expand their agricultural exports to China, further reducing the long-term competitiveness of American farmers.

These ripple effects extended to consumers, who faced higher prices on a wide range of goods. From electronics to clothing to everyday household items, the cost of living increased for millions of Americans as businesses passed on the additional costs of tariffs. For low-income households, which spend a larger share of their income on necessities, these price increases were particularly burdensome. The irony was hard to miss: policies touted as a means of helping American workers and families often ended up hurting them the most. The symbolism of tariffs as a tool for economic justice clashed with the reality of their regressive impact.

The uncertainty created by tariffs also had far-reaching consequences. Businesses thrive on stability, and the unpredictability of Trump's trade policies made long-term planning nearly impossible. Tariffs were announced, adjusted, and rescinded with little warning, leaving companies scrambling to adapt. This environment of uncertainty discouraged investment, as businesses hesitated to commit resources to new projects or expansions without a clear sense of the regulatory landscape. For industries that rely on global supply chains, the constant flux was particularly damaging, forcing companies to spend time and money on contingency plans rather than focusing on growth and innovation.

Internationally, the ripple effects of Trump's tariffs strained relationships with key allies and trading partners. Countries like Canada, Mexico, and the European Union, which had long been economic and political allies of the United States, were caught off guard by the administration's unilateral approach to trade policy. The imposition of tariffs on steel and aluminum from these countries, justified on dubious national security grounds, created resentment and led to retaliatory measures. These tit-for-tat escalations further disrupted global trade and weakened the multilateral institutions, such as the World Trade Organization (WTO), that have traditionally helped mediate trade disputes. The result was a more fragmented and volatile global economy, with long-term implications for America's leadership and influence on the world stage.

The ripple effects of tariffs also revealed the limits of symbolic policies in addressing systemic challenges. While tariffs were framed as a way to protect American workers and industries, they did little to address the root causes of economic insecurity. Stagnant wages, declining union power, and the lack of access to affordable education and healthcare remained pressing issues for millions of Americans, yet these challenges were sidelined in the broader conversation about trade. The focus on tariffs as a quick fix distracted from the need for comprehensive reforms that could create a more equitable and resilient economy.

One of the most troubling aspects of these ripple effects was the way they deepened existing inequalities. The benefits of tariffs, such as they were, tended to accrue to a narrow set of industries and corporations, while the costs were borne disproportionately by workers, small businesses, and consumers. This dynamic mirrored broader trends in the American economy, where the gains of growth have increasingly been concentrated at the top, leaving the majority of people with little to show for their efforts. By failing to address these structural inequalities, tariffs not only fell short of their promises but also perpetuated the very conditions they were supposed to alleviate.

The cultural and political consequences of the tariff ripple effect were equally significant. By framing trade policy as a battle between "us" and "them," the administration fostered a narrative of division and competition that undermined the potential for cooperation and solidarity. Domestically, this narrative pitted workers in different industries against one another, as some were seen as beneficiaries of tariffs while others bore their costs. Internationally, it created tensions with allies and trading partners, making it harder to build the collaborative relationships needed to address shared challenges like climate change, technological innovation, and global inequality.

Ultimately, the ripple effects of tariffs highlighted the dangers of relying on symbolic policies to address complex problems. While tariffs may have provided a temporary sense of action and control, their long-term impact was one of disruption, division, and missed opportunities. As the costs accumulated, it became clear that the promise of tariffs as a tool for economic renewal was an illusion, masking the need for deeper and more systemic reforms. The next section of this chapter will explore the lessons to be learned from these failures, focusing on the steps that can be taken to build a more inclusive and sustainable economy. The ripple effects of symbolic policies, as powerful as they may be, are not inevitable. By confronting the myths and misconceptions that sustain them, it is possible to chart a new course that prioritizes equity, resilience, and shared prosperity.

Part 3: The Path Forward: Beyond Symbolism to Substance

The failures of Trump's tariff policies and their far-reaching ripple effects illuminate a broader challenge in American governance: the tendency to rely on symbolic policies that prioritize short-term political gains over meaningful, long-term solutions. As the costs of tariffs mounted, rising consumer prices, strained global relationships, and deepening economic inequality, the illusion of their effectiveness became harder to sustain. Yet their failures also present an opportunity to rethink how America approaches economic policy, moving beyond the allure of simplistic fixes and toward strategies that genuinely address the systemic challenges facing the nation. This chapter explores how the lessons of the past can inform a path forward, one rooted in substance rather than symbolism.

To chart this new course, the first step is to acknowledge the interconnected nature of the modern economy. The globalized world cannot be navigated with isolationist tools like broad tariffs, which disrupt supply chains and strain international relationships. Instead, the U.S. must embrace its role in a global economy while working to ensure that globalization benefits a broader swath of the population. This means prioritizing trade agreements that include strong labor protections, environmental standards, and fair competition rules. It also requires a shift in focus from punishing other countries to empowering American workers through domestic investments and policy reforms.

Investing in Workers and Communities

One of the critical failures of the tariff approach was its inability to address the root causes of economic insecurity for American workers. While tariffs were framed as a way to protect jobs, they did little to reverse decades of wage stagnation, automation, and disinvestment in local communities. To build a more resilient economy, the U.S. must prioritize investments in education, job training, and infrastructure. These investments can equip workers with the skills needed to thrive in an economy increasingly driven by technology and innovation. Programs that support career transitions, such as retraining initiatives for workers displaced by automation or trade, are essential to ensuring that economic progress does not leave entire communities behind.

Equally important is addressing the decline of union power, which has played a significant role in the erosion of wages and job security. Strong labor protections and the revitalization of collective bargaining can help workers secure a fair share of the wealth they create. Policies that encourage unionization, such as repealing "right-to-work" laws and expanding protections for gig and contract workers, are critical to leveling the playing field and reducing income inequality. Unlike tariffs, which attempt to shield industries from external competition, these measures strengthen workers from within, giving them the tools to advocate for better conditions and opportunities.

Reforming the Tax and Trade System

The failure of tariffs also highlights the need for a more equitable tax and trade system. While tariffs function as a hidden tax on consumers, disproportionately affecting low-income households, a reformed tax system could more effectively address inequality and fund critical investments. Closing loopholes that allow corporations and the wealthy to avoid taxes, implementing higher rates on top earners, and introducing measures like a financial transactions tax could generate revenue to support social programs and infrastructure projects. These reforms would shift the burden of economic adjustment away from the working class and toward those with the greatest capacity to contribute.

In the realm of trade, the U.S. must move beyond the zero-sum thinking that has dominated recent debates. Instead of using tariffs as a blunt instrument, policymakers should focus on negotiating trade agreements that promote mutual benefits while addressing concerns like intellectual property theft and market access. Collaborative efforts with allies can amplify the U.S.'s leverage in addressing unfair trade practices, creating a more stable and cooperative global trade environment. Such agreements should prioritize sustainability and equity, ensuring that the benefits of trade are widely shared and that industries critical to national security and public welfare are protected.

Strengthening the Social Safety Net

Another key lesson from the failures of tariffs is the importance of a robust social safety net. The economic disruptions caused by the trade war underscored the vulnerability of workers and families who lack access to affordable healthcare, childcare, and housing. Strengthening these supports can provide a buffer against the shocks of economic change, whether from trade disputes, automation, or other forces. Expanding access to Medicaid, enacting universal childcare programs, and investing in affordable housing are not just moral imperatives; they are also economic ones, creating the stability needed for individuals and communities to thrive.

Policies like a universal basic income (UBI) or expanded unemployment benefits could also play a role in reducing economic precarity. While controversial, these measures acknowledge the reality that not all workers displaced by economic changes will find equivalent employment. Providing a guaranteed income floor ensures that all citizens have the resources to meet basic needs, reducing the strain on local economies and creating a foundation for broader prosperity. Such policies represent a shift away from the punitive approach of tariffs and toward one that emphasizes shared responsibility and collective resilience.

Rebuilding Trust and Accountability

For any of these reforms to succeed, there must be a restoration of trust in government and economic institutions. The failures of tariffs, and the broader reliance on symbolic policies, have eroded public confidence in policymakers' ability to act in the public interest. Transparency and accountability are essential to rebuilding this trust. Policymakers must be clear about the goals and expected outcomes of economic policies, using evidence-based approaches to design and evaluate their impact. When policies fail to deliver, admitting mistakes and adjusting course is crucial to maintaining credibility.

Public engagement is another critical component of rebuilding trust. Too often, economic policy is shaped by elite interests, with little input from the communities most affected by its outcomes. Creating mechanisms for meaningful public participation, such as citizen advisory boards or town hall forums, can help ensure that policies reflect the needs and priorities of ordinary Americans. This participatory approach also fosters a sense of ownership and agency, countering the disillusionment that has fueled political polarization and cynicism.

A New Narrative for Economic Policy

Perhaps the most important step in moving beyond the failures of tariffs is the creation of a new narrative for economic policy. The myth of economic independence, while powerful, is fundamentally at odds with the realities of a globalized world. A more constructive narrative would emphasize the interconnectedness of nations and the potential for shared prosperity. This narrative must acknowledge the challenges of globalization while highlighting its opportunities, framing international cooperation as a means of addressing common goals like climate change, technological innovation, and social equity.

At the same time, this new narrative must celebrate the value of collective action at home. The ideal of the self-made individual, while inspiring, often obscures the role of community, government, and shared resources in creating opportunities for success. By shifting the focus from individualism to interdependence, policymakers can build a narrative that resonates with the values of fairness, inclusion, and mutual support. This narrative is not about abandoning American exceptionalism but redefining it to reflect the nation's potential to lead by example in creating a more just and sustainable global economy.

The failures of Trump's tariffs and the broader reliance on symbolic policies offer a stark reminder of the dangers of prioritizing rhetoric over results. Yet they also provide an opportunity to chart a new course, one that moves beyond the illusions of strength and independence and toward a more inclusive and resilient economy. By investing in workers and communities, reforming the tax and trade system, strengthening the social safety net, and rebuilding trust in government, the U.S. can create a foundation for shared prosperity in the 21st century. This path forward requires not just policy changes but a cultural shift, embracing the values of cooperation, accountability, and shared responsibility. The costs of inaction are too high to ignore, and the potential rewards of a more equitable and sustainable economy are too great to pass up. It is time to move beyond the failures of the past and build a future that works for everyone.

The $4,000 Breakdown: How Tariffs Add Up

While the leopard's appetite may be metaphorical, the costs to American households are very real. Tariffs, essentially taxes on imports, increase the prices of everyday goods by raising costs for businesses, who then pass those costs on to consumers. Economists estimate that Trump's tariffs cost the average U.S. household $4,000 per year, based on increased prices across several key categories. Here's how those costs break down:

1. Food and Groceries
Examples: Soy-based products, meat (pork, beef), produce.
Impact: Retaliatory tariffs from China and the EU targeted U.S. agricultural exports. Farmers faced declining revenue, and bailout payments didn't cover the gap. This drove up prices for domestic goods.
Estimated cost increase: $400/year.

2. Electronics
Examples: Smartphones, laptops, TVs.
Impact: Tariffs on Chinese imports affected tech components, increasing retail prices by 10–25%. With no alternative suppliers, companies passed costs to consumers.
Estimated cost increase: $500/year.

3. Appliances and Home Goods
Examples: Washing machines, refrigerators, furniture.
Impact: Steel and aluminum tariffs raised production costs, while tariffs on finished goods made imported appliances more expensive.
Estimated cost increase: $350/year.

4. Clothing and Footwear
Examples: Shoes, apparel, accessories.
Impact: Tariffs targeted textiles and finished goods from China, raising costs for retailers who relied on low-cost imports. These costs trickled down to consumers.
Estimated cost increase: $200/year.

5. Automobiles and Repairs
Examples: Cars, auto parts, tires.
Impact: Tariffs on steel, aluminum, and imported auto parts raised prices on vehicles and repairs. Repair shops had to adjust labor costs accordingly.
Estimated cost increase: $600/year.

6. Everyday Goods
Examples: Household items (cleaning supplies, kitchenware), tools, toys.
Impact: Broad tariffs on consumer goods created price hikes on items that are staples for families.
Estimated cost increase: $500/year.

7. Energy Costs
Examples: Gasoline, home heating oil.
Impact: Retaliatory tariffs affected energy exports and led to higher prices for domestic energy. Transportation costs for goods also increased.
Estimated cost increase: $300/year.

Total: $4,000 Annually

The leopard doesn't discriminate when it feasts. From groceries to gadgets, tariffs create a stealth tax that hits every household budget. And while the rhetoric painted tariffs as a patriotic policy, the reality was clear: Americans paid the bill, one inflated price tag at a time.

Chapter 6
Another Great Leopard Wealth Giveaway

Part 1: *Another* Transfer of Wealth from the Bottom to the Top

To estimate how tariffs might increase the wealth of the already wealthy, such as the top 1%, we need to consider indirect mechanisms, such as corporate profit redistribution and asset price increases, rather than direct wealth transfers. Here's an outline of how tariffs might disproportionately benefit the wealthiest:

1. Corporate Profits and Stock Market Gains

Pass-Through of Costs to Consumers: Large corporations with market power often pass the increased costs of tariffs onto consumers through higher prices, protecting their profit margins. These corporations are predominantly owned by wealthy shareholders, including the top 1%.

Domestic Price Increases: Tariffs reduce competition by making imports more expensive. Domestic producers often capitalize on this by raising their prices, boosting profit margins, which translates into higher stock valuations.

Stock Ownership Concentration: The wealthiest 1% own a significant proportion of U.S. stocks (over 50% of equities). Thus, any increase in stock prices due to higher corporate profits or market dominance directly benefits them.

2. Government Subsidies and Bailouts

Agricultural and Corporate Aid Programs: Programs like the $28 billion farm bailout funded by tariffs were disproportionately directed to large agribusinesses, many of which are owned or controlled by wealthy individuals or conglomerates. These subsidies effectively shield the wealthy from losses while smaller players suffer.

Supply Chain Shifts Favor Big Business: Larger corporations have the resources to restructure supply chains to minimize tariff impacts. Smaller businesses cannot compete as effectively, leading to market consolidation, which benefits dominant players and their wealthy owners.

3. Economic Inequality and Wealth Redistribution

Higher Consumer Costs: Tariffs act as a regressive tax, disproportionately affecting low- and middle-income households, who spend more of their income on goods subject to tariffs. This reduces disposable income for the majority while enabling corporations to extract higher revenues.

Wealth Concentration: As profits flow to top executives and shareholders, inequality grows. For example, major corporations that navigated the tariffs profitably distributed billions in stock buybacks during the trade war, a move that directly enriches shareholders.

Hypothetical Example: Quantifying the Impact
Let's assume:
$80 billion in tariff revenue collected annually (2019 U.S. tariff income estimate).

A portion of this revenue (via price increases) is redistributed as corporate profits. If 20% of these costs are absorbed by the wealthiest corporations, that's $16 billion in additional profit.

Wealth Ownership Effect: With the top 1% owning ~50% of corporate assets, $8 billion of this increase accrues to them annually.

This figure doesn't include compounding effects from stock market gains, government aid to large firms, or supply chain restructuring advantages. Including these, the wealth accruing to the 1% due to tariffs could plausibly reach tens of billions annually.

Part 2: Detailed Breakdown: How Tariffs Increase the Wealth of the Top 1%

This analysis explores the pathways through which tariffs boost the wealth of the top 1% through corporate profits, market dominance, and financial asset appreciation. Here's a hypothetical breakdown using real-world industries as examples.

1. Corporate Profits and Stock Market Gains
Industry Example: Consumer Electronics

Tariff Impact: A 25% tariff is imposed on imported electronics, such as smartphones and laptops.

Corporate Response: Major companies like Apple or Dell can pass on these costs to consumers, increasing prices by 10-20% while retaining most of their profit margins.

Stock Ownership: The top 1% own a significant portion of shares in these tech giants. Higher profits from price increases lead to higher stock valuations.

Wealth Redistribution Effect: If the total market for imported electronics is $150 billion annually and 20% of the tariff costs ($7.5 billion) translate into additional profits for corporations, the top 1%, owning ~50% of the equity, gain $3.75 billion from just this industry.

2. Market Consolidation
Industry Example: Agricultural Products
Tariff Impact: China retaliates against U.S. tariffs by imposing tariffs on American soybeans and pork, cutting demand for small- and mid-sized farmers.

Corporate Response: Large agribusinesses like Archer Daniels Midland and Cargill, which have diversified global supply chains, acquire distressed farms and consolidate control over the market.

Subsidy Effect: Of the $28 billion farm bailout, a significant portion goes to large agribusinesses, further strengthening their position.

Wealth Redistribution Effect: Assume 60% ($16.8 billion) of the bailout goes to major agribusinesses owned by the wealthiest individuals or entities. The top 1%, with their concentrated ownership stakes, accrue an estimated $8.4 billion from these government subsidies.

3. Stock Buybacks and Dividend Increases
Industry Example: Steel and Aluminum

Tariff Impact: A 25% tariff on imported steel and 10% on aluminum boosts prices for domestic producers.

Corporate Response: Domestic steel companies, like U.S. Steel and Nucor, increase their profits due to reduced competition from imports. Instead of reinvesting in worker wages or infrastructure, they allocate profits to stock buybacks.

Stock Buyback Effect: In 2019, Nucor announced $2 billion in stock buybacks. Assuming similar patterns across the steel industry, billions flow back to shareholders.

Wealth Redistribution Effect: With the top 1% owning over 50% of equities, they capture at least $1 billion in wealth directly from these buybacks.

4. Increased Market Power in Retail
Industry Example: Apparel and Retail

Tariff Impact: A 10-25% tariff on imported clothing and textiles raises costs for all retailers.

Corporate Response: Large chains like Walmart and Amazon shift production to non-tariffed countries or negotiate better terms with suppliers, whereas smaller competitors cannot adapt and go out of business.

Wealth Redistribution Effect: As smaller businesses close, larger corporations gain market share, boosting revenues and profits. If Walmart's market share increases by 5%, leading to $10 billion in additional annual revenue, and a 10% profit margin, the $1 billion profit increase is heavily concentrated among the top 1% who hold Walmart stock.

Broader Considerations

Stock Market Effects: Rising corporate profits from tariff-inflated prices increase broader equity market valuations. If tariffs contribute to a 5% increase in S&P 500 value (estimated $1.2 trillion gain in market cap), the top 1%, holding ~50% of these equities, capture $600 billion.

Compounding Gains: Wealth invested in equities grows exponentially, meaning the long-term gains for the top 1% far exceed immediate profits.

Part 3: The Leopard's True Feast: Tariffs as Wealth Transfer Mechanisms

When tariffs are imposed, they are often framed as patriotic measures to protect the national economy and ensure fair competition. However, this framing obscures the fact that tariffs are essentially taxes on imports, costs that are inevitably passed down to consumers. The wealthy, with their diversified income streams and ability to absorb financial fluctuations, are relatively insulated from these increases. For low- and middle-income households, however, the story is starkly different.

Tariffs drive up the prices of goods, from groceries to electronics, creating what economists term a "regressive tax." The burden of this regressive tax disproportionately falls on households that spend a larger share of their income on essentials. For example, when tariffs on steel and aluminum raise production costs for items like cars and appliances, those costs are absorbed not by corporate executives but by the consumers buying these products. A family scraping to save for a new refrigerator or car repair is hit far harder than an executive whose bonuses remain untouched.

Even as consumers pay more, businesses reliant on imports face higher costs, forcing them to make tough decisions: raise prices, cut wages, or downsize. These dynamics ripple through the economy, reducing disposable income for most households while driving increased profits for corporations that can exploit loopholes or adjust their supply chains. The result is a system that effectively redistributes wealth from the bottom up.

The Bailout Pipeline: Subsidizing the Elite

A key feature of the Trump administration's trade war was the introduction of bailout programs intended to cushion the impact of retaliatory tariffs, particularly for farmers. While these payments were presented as aid to struggling agricultural communities, the reality was far more inequitable. A disproportionate share of the $28 billion in bailout funds flowed to large agribusinesses rather than small family farms, many of which were already teetering on the brink of collapse.

The structure of these bailouts mirrored the broader economic favoritism baked into the system. Large agribusinesses, with their economies of scale and access to lobbying resources, were better equipped to navigate the complexities of federal aid. Meanwhile, smaller farms, which relied more heavily on direct exports to affected markets, faced financial ruin. For every billion-dollar agribusiness bolstered by the bailout, there were countless smaller farms forced into foreclosure. The bailout effectively became a wealth transfer mechanism, using taxpayer dollars to shield corporate agribusinesses from the fallout of trade policies while leaving small farmers to fend for themselves.

This dynamic is not unique to agriculture. In industries like manufacturing, corporations with global supply chains often managed to circumvent tariff impacts by sourcing from non-tariffed regions or passing costs onto consumers. Small businesses, without such flexibility, bore the brunt of these costs, leading to closures and layoffs that further concentrated market power in the hands of larger corporations.

Supply Chain Realignments: Profiting From Chaos

One of the less visible ways tariffs transfer wealth upward is through supply chain realignments. Large multinational corporations often have the resources to shift their production or sourcing to countries not affected by tariffs, allowing them to maintain profit margins while their smaller competitors flounder. For example, while tariffs on Chinese goods were intended to pressure Beijing, many large companies responded by relocating manufacturing to Vietnam, Mexico, or other nations outside the tariff regime.

These shifts, while touted as evidence of corporate adaptability, highlight a profound inequality in the economic system. Smaller firms, which lack the capital to quickly reconfigure supply chains, are forced to absorb higher costs or shut down entirely. Meanwhile, the corporations that can adapt reap the benefits of reduced competition and increased market share.

The Financial Sector: Betting on the Tariff Game

Another less-discussed aspect of tariffs is their impact on the financial sector. For hedge funds and institutional investors, the volatility created by tariff announcements provides lucrative opportunities for speculation. Market fluctuations tied to trade policy shifts allow the wealthy to profit through stock trading, currency speculation, and commodity markets.

The financial elite's ability to capitalize on tariff-induced chaos stands in stark contrast to the experiences of ordinary workers

and businesses, who face heightened uncertainty and financial
precarity. While small manufacturers struggle to cope with
rising input costs, investors bet on their demise. This dynamic
underscores how tariffs, far from harming the elite, create new
avenues for wealth accumulation at the expense of the broader
economy.

Consolidating Wealth and Power

The systemic nature of tariffs as wealth transfer mechanisms is
rooted in the broader dynamics of economic inequality. Policies
that claim to protect domestic industries often have the opposite
effect, favoring consolidation over competition. As small
businesses are driven out by rising costs and larger corporations
solidify their dominance, the concentration of wealth and power
becomes self-reinforcing.

The tech sector offers a stark example. While tariffs raised prices
on consumer electronics, large tech firms with diversified
revenue streams and offshore operations saw their valuations
soar. The very policies that were supposed to curb dependency
on foreign manufacturing often ended up enriching the same
corporations that had offshored jobs in the first place.

Tariffs as a Political Tool: Who Benefits?

Perhaps the most insidious aspect of tariffs is their use as a
political tool to create the appearance of economic action. By
framing tariffs as a means of "standing up" to foreign
adversaries, policymakers deflect attention from systemic
domestic issues like wage stagnation, healthcare access, and
corporate tax avoidance. This sleight of hand benefits the
political and economic elite, who leverage nationalist rhetoric to
distract from policies that perpetuate inequality.

The wealthiest Americans, who own the majority of stocks and benefit from corporate tax cuts, have seen their net worths soar even as tariffs disrupted the broader economy. This disparity reveals the true beneficiaries of policies ostensibly designed to protect the working class.

Tariffs, for all their patriotic rhetoric, are a modern iteration of a longstanding economic trend: policies that exploit the many to enrich the few. The leopard's feast is not an accident but a feature of a system that prioritizes short-term gains and entrenched privilege over equity and resilience. As consumers shoulder the hidden tax of tariffs, small businesses face closures, and corporations consolidate power, the true cost of these policies becomes clear. Tariffs are not just a flawed economic tool; they are a mechanism for sustaining and deepening systemic inequalities.

JUSTICE AND EQUALITY

Chapter 7
The Alternatives – Leopards vs. Common Sense

Part 1: Paths Forward – Breaking Free from the Tariff Trap

The conversation around trade in America has long been dominated by simplistic narratives that cast the global economy as a battlefield and tariffs as the ultimate weapon of self-defense. This approach, while politically expedient, is both reductive and harmful, perpetuating a cycle of reactionary policies that fail to address the underlying challenges of globalization. To chart a new course, the United States must move beyond the false promises of tariffs and embrace trade policies rooted in fairness, collaboration, and long-term investment. These alternatives are not just theoretical, they have been successfully implemented in past administrations and offer a roadmap for a more equitable and resilient economic future.

A foundational element of alternative trade policies is the rejection of unilateralism in favor of collaborative agreements that reflect shared interests and values. One of the most notable examples is the trade policy approach under the Clinton administration, which championed the North American Free Trade Agreement (NAFTA). While NAFTA has been criticized for its shortcomings, it also represented a critical step in establishing a framework for regional economic integration. By reducing barriers to trade and investment among the United States, Canada, and Mexico, NAFTA facilitated economic growth and created opportunities for cross-border collaboration. Its shortcomings, such as inadequate labor and environmental protections, offer lessons for crafting better agreements in the future rather than abandoning the concept altogether.

The Obama administration further demonstrated the potential of multilateral agreements with its pursuit of the Trans-Pacific Partnership (TPP). The TPP was designed to establish high standards for trade and investment across a diverse group of nations, addressing issues such as labor rights, environmental protections, and intellectual property enforcement. While the agreement faced political opposition and was ultimately abandoned, its framework highlighted the importance of setting rules that promote fairness and accountability in global trade. A revitalized commitment to such agreements, with adjustments to address legitimate concerns, could position the United States as a leader in shaping a more equitable global economy.

In addition to collaborative trade agreements, domestic investment is a crucial pillar of any successful trade policy. Tariffs, by raising costs for consumers and businesses, often undermine the very industries they claim to protect. In contrast, targeted investments in infrastructure, education, and research can strengthen the foundation of the economy and enhance its competitiveness on the global stage. The American Recovery and Reinvestment Act (ARRA) of 2009, enacted under the Obama administration, provides a clear example of how such investments can stimulate growth. By allocating funds to modernize transportation networks, expand broadband access, and support clean energy initiatives, the ARRA not only created jobs but also laid the groundwork for long-term economic resilience.

A forward-thinking trade policy must also prioritize the needs of workers and communities that have been left behind by globalization. The narrative that trade agreements inherently harm American workers ignores the broader context of economic change, including the role of automation, corporate consolidation, and declining union power. Addressing these challenges requires policies that go beyond trade itself, such as strengthening labor protections, raising the minimum wage, and supporting collective bargaining. The Biden administration's focus on infrastructure investment and green energy jobs represents a step in this direction, signaling a commitment to creating opportunities for workers in emerging industries.

Environmental sustainability is another critical dimension of modern trade policy. The global economy is undergoing a transition toward low-carbon technologies, and the United States must position itself as a leader in this shift. Trade agreements that include enforceable environmental standards can play a key role in driving this transition, incentivizing innovation and reducing the carbon footprint of global supply chains. At the same time, domestic policies such as tax credits for renewable energy projects and investments in clean technology research can ensure that American industries remain competitive in a changing landscape.

Addressing income inequality is essential to the success of any trade policy. The benefits of globalization have often been concentrated among the wealthiest segments of society, while low- and middle-income households bear the costs. This dynamic is exacerbated by tariffs, which act as a regressive tax on consumers. To counteract this, trade policy must be accompanied by measures that promote equity, such as progressive taxation, expanded access to affordable healthcare, and robust social safety nets. These policies not only reduce economic disparities but also build public support for trade by ensuring that its benefits are widely shared.

The role of technology and innovation cannot be overstated in shaping the future of trade. Advances in artificial intelligence, automation, and digital connectivity are transforming industries and creating new opportunities for economic growth. However, these changes also pose challenges, particularly for workers in sectors that are highly susceptible to disruption. To harness the potential of technology while mitigating its risks, the United States must invest in education and training programs that prepare workers for the jobs of the future. Initiatives such as coding bootcamps, STEM scholarships, and partnerships between businesses and community colleges can help bridge the skills gap and ensure that the workforce is equipped to thrive in a rapidly evolving economy.

The international dimension of trade policy extends beyond economic considerations to issues of geopolitics and national security. In an interconnected world, the stability and prosperity of the United States are closely linked to those of its trading partners. Strengthening alliances through trade agreements can enhance cooperation on issues such as climate change, cybersecurity, and public health. For example, a renewed commitment to the Paris Agreement on climate change, coupled with trade policies that incentivize sustainable practices, can demonstrate global leadership and foster goodwill among nations. Similarly, initiatives to address supply chain vulnerabilities, such as diversifying sources of critical materials, can bolster resilience and reduce reliance on adversarial powers.

Ultimately, the success of alternative trade policies depends on the willingness of policymakers to engage in honest and transparent dialogue with the public. The rhetoric of tariffs often appeals to emotions and fears, painting a simplistic picture of economic competition that obscures the complexities of global trade. By contrast, a forward-looking approach requires clear communication about the challenges and opportunities of globalization. Policymakers must articulate a vision of trade that emphasizes shared prosperity and addresses the legitimate concerns of workers and businesses. This includes acknowledging past mistakes, such as the neglect of communities impacted by economic transitions, and committing to policies that leave no one behind.

In rejecting the tariff trap and embracing collaborative, equitable, and sustainable trade policies, the United States can chart a path toward a more prosperous and inclusive future. The leopard of reactionary trade policy thrives on division and short-term thinking, but it is not invincible. By focusing on investments that build resilience, agreements that promote fairness, and policies that empower workers, the nation can rise above the false choices of the past and embrace a vision of trade that benefits all. This is not merely a matter of economic necessity, it is a moral imperative, one that reflects the values of fairness, opportunity, and cooperation that define the American ideal.

In Part 2, we will delve into what a cooperative trade framework could look like in practice. We'll explore strategies that prioritize mutual benefit over conflict, from rethinking trade agreements to investing in domestic industries and workers. By examining successful policies from past administrations and identifying new opportunities for global collaboration, we will outline how trade can serve as a tool for equity and resilience, rather than division and exploitation. The road ahead is challenging, but it offers a path toward an economy that works not just for the few, but for everyone.

Part 2: Reimagining Trade – Cooperation Over Conflict

The failures of protectionism, while stark, offer a critical opportunity to redefine the United States' approach to global trade. The concept of cooperation over conflict is not a naïve aspiration but a pragmatic necessity in an interconnected world. For decades, the U.S. has been both a leader and participant in trade agreements designed to foster economic growth, innovation, and mutual benefit. However, the breakdown of trust in these systems, whether through mismanagement, political opportunism, or genuine flaws, has paved the way for divisive policies like tariffs. To move forward, the U.S. must revisit the core principles of cooperative trade, learning from both past successes and failures, to build a resilient, equitable global economy.

The first step in reimagining trade is to acknowledge the global nature of modern supply chains. Unlike in the mid-20th century, when domestic manufacturing dominated the economy, today's goods are rarely produced within a single nation's borders. A smartphone assembled in Asia relies on components from multiple continents, with design, raw materials, and production involving dozens of countries. Policies that attempt to disrupt these intricate networks, such as blanket tariffs, ignore the economic realities of this interconnected system. Instead of penalizing foreign partners, the U.S. should focus on strengthening the domestic contributions to these supply chains. This could involve investing in advanced manufacturing technologies, fostering innovation hubs, and ensuring that workers are equipped with the skills necessary to thrive in these industries.

One instructive example comes from the Obama administration's focus on renewable energy partnerships. By emphasizing investment in clean energy technologies and fostering international cooperation, the U.S. positioned itself as a leader in a rapidly growing industry. Programs like ARPA-E, which supported groundbreaking energy research, demonstrated how public investment could spur innovation while encouraging private sector growth. Moreover, partnerships with countries like Germany and Japan in developing solar and wind technologies highlighted the benefits of collaborative trade. These initiatives not only strengthened domestic industries but also created jobs and reduced the economic dependence on volatile fossil fuel markets.

Similarly, the Clinton administration's approach to trade provides a valuable template. The North American Free Trade Agreement (NAFTA), while not without its critics, showcased the potential for regional trade agreements to drive mutual prosperity. By reducing barriers to trade among the U.S., Canada, and Mexico, NAFTA facilitated the growth of industries reliant on cross-border supply chains, such as automotive manufacturing. However, the agreement also revealed the necessity of accompanying trade liberalization with policies that protect and empower workers. The failure to address labor displacement and wage stagnation in certain sectors created resentment and backlash, underscoring the need for comprehensive strategies that include robust safety nets, retraining programs, and labor protections.

A reimagined trade policy must also prioritize equity and sustainability. Trade agreements should include enforceable standards on labor rights, environmental protections, and corporate accountability. This approach not only ensures fair competition but also addresses some of the root causes of economic inequality. For example, provisions requiring multinational corporations to adhere to minimum wage and workplace safety standards in all countries of operation could help reduce the exploitation of low-wage workers while leveling the playing field for domestic industries. Similarly, integrating environmental safeguards into trade agreements can promote sustainable development and mitigate the impact of climate change, a pressing global challenge that demands coordinated action.

One work-in-progress example was the Trans-Pacific Partnership (TPP), a trade deal that, while controversial and widely criticized for potentially offshoring jobs and undermining domestic industries, included provisions for progressive labor and environmental standards. The agreement faced significant backlash for prioritizing corporate interests and failing to adequately safeguard against economic harm to certain American workers, yet it also offered a glimpse of how trade deals could be structured to address broader social and environmental goals with the right adjustments. The U.S. ultimately withdrew from the TPP under the Trump administration, but with substantial reforms, such as stronger protections for workers, stricter enforcement mechanisms, and clearer safeguards against job outsourcing, its framework could serve as a foundation for more equitable and sustainable trade agreements. Re-engaging with multilateral agreements, if done carefully and with significant revisions, could allow the U.S. to lead in shaping global trade rules while addressing shared challenges like intellectual property theft, labor exploitation, and climate change.

In addition to shaping international trade rules, domestic investment must play a central role in reimagining economic policy. Infrastructure development, for instance, offers a dual benefit: it strengthens the foundation for economic growth while creating well-paying jobs. From modernizing transportation networks to expanding broadband access, investments in infrastructure can enhance the competitiveness of American businesses while addressing regional disparities in economic opportunity. Similarly, supporting small and medium-sized enterprises (SMEs) through grants, low-interest loans, and technical assistance can empower local economies and reduce reliance on volatile global markets.

Another critical area for domestic investment is education and workforce development. The rapid pace of technological change requires a workforce that is adaptable and skilled in emerging industries. Expanding access to vocational training, apprenticeships, and community college programs can ensure that workers are prepared for the jobs of the future. Policies that support lifelong learning, such as subsidized retraining programs for displaced workers, can help mitigate the disruptions caused by economic transitions. These investments not only benefit individual workers but also strengthen the overall economy by enhancing productivity and innovation.

Reimagining trade also involves addressing the role of corporate accountability. In recent decades, globalization has often been accompanied by the erosion of corporate responsibility, as companies exploit loopholes to evade taxes, suppress wages, and prioritize short-term profits over long-term sustainability. Trade policies must include measures to curb these practices, such as closing tax havens, enforcing anti-monopoly regulations, and requiring corporations to disclose their environmental and social impacts. By holding companies accountable, the U.S. can ensure that the benefits of trade are distributed more equitably and that economic growth is aligned with broader social goals.

Perhaps the most significant shift required in reimagining trade is the recognition that economic policy cannot be separated from broader issues of social and environmental justice. Addressing income inequality, racial disparities, and climate change is not just a moral imperative but an economic one. Policies that promote inclusivity and sustainability create a stronger, more resilient economy capable of withstanding global challenges. Trade agreements should be viewed as tools to advance these goals, rather than as isolated instruments of economic strategy.

As we transition into Part 3, we will explore how these principles of cooperative trade and domestic investment can be translated into actionable policies. By examining case studies from both the U.S. and other nations, we will identify specific strategies for building a trade framework that prioritizes fairness, resilience, and shared prosperity. From innovative financing mechanisms to grassroots labor movements, Part 3 will outline the practical steps needed to implement a reimagined approach to trade. The question is no longer whether the U.S. can afford to embrace change, but whether it can afford not to.

Part 3: Charting a New Course for Trade Policy

As the failures of tariffs and isolationist policies become increasingly apparent, the United States faces a critical opportunity to redefine its trade policy for the 21st century. Moving away from the false promise of protectionism requires embracing a nuanced, equitable, and forward-looking approach that prioritizes the well-being of workers and the environment alongside economic growth. This shift demands a recalibration of both the philosophy and the mechanics of trade agreements, ensuring that they are not just instruments of corporate profit but tools for fostering shared prosperity and resilience in a globalized world.

At the heart of this recalibration is the need to reimagine the United States' role as a leader in the global economy. Leadership in trade cannot rely on punitive tariffs or unilateral demands; it requires building trust, fostering collaboration, and setting an example. A successful trade policy must actively engage with allies and trading partners to develop agreements that balance open markets with protections for vulnerable industries, labor standards, and environmental safeguards. The potential for such a model is already visible in efforts like the updated United States-Mexico-Canada Agreement (USMCA), which included provisions for labor rights and fair wages, albeit modest ones. Expanding and refining these elements in future agreements could make trade a driver of economic justice rather than a source of inequality.

Another pillar of this new trade policy must be investment in domestic resilience. The hollowing out of American manufacturing and the decline of middle-class jobs are not solely the result of trade agreements but reflect decades of underinvestment in critical infrastructure, education, and technological innovation. A robust industrial policy that includes targeted investments in green energy, advanced manufacturing, and high-tech industries can create high-quality jobs and reduce reliance on foreign imports. For example, incentives for reshoring industries, combined with workforce training programs, can ensure that American workers are equipped to thrive in a competitive global market. This strategy also aligns with addressing climate change, as domestic investments in renewable energy and sustainable production methods can set a global standard for environmental responsibility.

In tandem with fostering domestic industries, the United States must pursue trade agreements that reflect 21st-century priorities. This means addressing not only traditional concerns like tariffs and market access but also pressing issues such as digital trade, data privacy, and climate adaptation. Agreements that include enforceable standards for emissions reductions, renewable energy investment, and the protection of natural resources can transform trade into a lever for global environmental progress. Likewise, digital trade policies that protect consumers' data and promote equitable access to technology can position the United States as a leader in the rapidly evolving digital economy.

Transparency and accountability are crucial to rebuilding public trust in trade policy. Too often, trade agreements have been negotiated behind closed doors, fueling perceptions that they serve elite interests at the expense of ordinary workers. Engaging with stakeholders, labor unions, environmental groups, small businesses, and local communities, throughout the negotiation process can ensure that agreements reflect a broader range of interests. This participatory approach can also help counter the fear and skepticism that have long plagued discussions of globalization, making the benefits of trade more tangible and widely understood.

Finally, a modern trade policy must include a robust safety net for workers and communities affected by economic transitions. While trade creates opportunities, it also displaces industries and workers, often disproportionately impacting already vulnerable populations. Programs that provide income support, job retraining, and community reinvestment can mitigate these effects and ensure that no group is left behind. Policies like wage insurance, expanded unemployment benefits, and regional economic development initiatives can help workers adapt to change without falling into economic insecurity.

The road to a more equitable and effective trade policy will not be without challenges. Political polarization, corporate lobbying, and global economic instability all pose significant obstacles. However, the alternative, clinging to a model of trade that prioritizes short-term gains and punitive measures, risks further economic stagnation, environmental degradation, and geopolitical isolation. By embracing collaboration, fairness, and forward-thinking investment, the United States can not only reclaim its position as a leader in global trade but also build a more resilient and inclusive economy at home.

In conclusion, the path forward lies in rejecting the simplistic allure of protectionism and tariffs in favor of a comprehensive strategy that addresses the root causes of economic insecurity and inequality. Trade policy must evolve to meet the complexities of the modern world, balancing the needs of workers, the environment, and innovation with the imperatives of growth and competition. The time has come to turn the page on outdated approaches and chart a new course, one guided by common sense, shared prosperity, and a commitment to a sustainable and equitable future.

Chapter 8
Why Leopards Always Eat the Poor

Part 1: The Leopard's Dinner Bell

If there's one rule we've learned about economic policy, it's this: when politicians promise they're helping the "little guy," you better double-check whose pocket they're actually lining. Trump's tariffs were no exception. They were sold as a patriotic tool to rebuild America's manufacturing glory days, to stick it to China, and to protect hardworking American families. But instead of reviving factories and boosting wages, these tariffs quietly handed the check to regular folks while the richest Americans continued feasting. It turns out, when the leopard gets hungry, it's not heading to the gated communities. It's stalking middle- and low-income households, who can't outrun the price hikes and job losses it brings.

Let's start with the obvious: tariffs are a tax, plain and simple. You can dress them up in nationalist rhetoric or tough-on-China soundbites, but at the end of the day, tariffs make things more expensive. When Trump slapped tariffs on steel, aluminum, and hundreds of billions of dollars' worth of Chinese imports, it didn't take long for the costs to hit consumers. Prices went up on everything from cars to canned goods, appliances to electronics. Companies that relied on those imported materials and products didn't just eat the extra cost, they passed it down the line. And guess who's at the end of the line? Regular Americans trying to stretch their paychecks.

For families already living paycheck to paycheck, those price increases weren't just inconvenient, they were devastating. When your grocery bill jumps because imported soy or pork got caught in a trade war crossfire, it's not the billionaires who feel the pinch. When the cost of a new washing machine spikes because of steel tariffs, it's not Wall Street execs who have to

107

decide between appliance repairs and rent. The reality is, tariffs hit the poor and working-class hardest because a bigger share of their income goes toward essentials. This is what economists call regressive taxation. But you don't need a fancy term to understand that when prices go up, the people with less money to spare are the first to feel the pain.

And it wasn't just consumer goods. Industries that depended on affordable materials, like auto manufacturers, construction companies, and small retailers, faced higher costs too. Some raised their prices to cover the difference, passing it along to customers. Others couldn't compete and shut their doors, laying off workers in the process. The ripple effects hit communities across the country, especially those already struggling with job losses and economic decline. This wasn't the promised renaissance of American manufacturing, it was economic whiplash, with workers bearing the brunt of a policy they were told would protect them.

Now, here's where it gets infuriating: while working families were watching their budgets stretch to the breaking point, the wealthiest Americans were doing just fine. You see, the real genius of these tariff policies wasn't in their execution, it was in the way they were paired with a broader economic agenda that funneled even more money to the top. Take the Trump tax cuts of 2017, for example. These cuts slashed corporate tax rates and handed massive breaks to the wealthiest Americans, even as the middle and lower classes saw only modest benefits, if they saw any at all. The result? A ballooning deficit and an even wider wealth gap. The tariffs might have been grabbing headlines, but the real magic trick was happening behind the scenes, where the rich were getting richer, and everyone else was left holding the bag.

Here's how it all ties together: tariffs raised the cost of living for ordinary people, while corporate tax cuts ensured that the wealthiest individuals and companies were shielded from those same financial pressures. The big players could afford to move production overseas to avoid tariffs altogether. Small businesses and American workers? Not so much. They were stuck with higher prices, fewer opportunities, and a government that seemed more interested in photo ops than real solutions. It's like throwing crumbs to the people on the ground while the folks in the ivory tower feast, and then asking the ones on the ground to pick up the bill.

And let's not forget the farmers. If anyone should've been front and center in Trump's America-first policies, it was rural agricultural communities. But instead, they found themselves in the crosshairs of retaliatory tariffs from countries like China, who slapped tariffs on American soybeans, pork, and other key exports. Overnight, farmers lost access to their biggest markets. Prices tanked, crops rotted, and family farms teetered on the edge of collapse. The government tried to soften the blow with bailout programs, but these payouts often went to the biggest agribusinesses rather than the family farms most in need. So while the trade war raged on, many small farmers were left asking, "Whose side is the government really on?"

The whole thing becomes even more enraging when you realize how avoidable it was. Economists across the spectrum warned that tariffs wouldn't bring back jobs or manufacturing, that they'd hurt consumers and alienate our trade partners. But those warnings were drowned out by the drumbeat of nationalist rhetoric. Trump's base was told this was about fighting for American workers, standing up to foreign competition, and rebuilding the heartland. In reality, it was about political theater, projecting strength while enacting policies that ultimately benefited the wealthy and well-connected. The leopard was eating the poor, and the cheering crowds didn't even realize they were next.

As we wrap up this first part, it's clear that tariffs were never about protecting the little guy. They were a convenient tool to shift the burden of economic policies onto those least able to bear it, all while rewarding the very top. But tariffs are just one

piece of a much larger puzzle. In Part 2, we'll dig deeper into
the broader Republican playbook, the one that's turned
regressive taxation and wealth inequality into a political art
form. From tax cuts to deregulation, these policies have
consistently prioritized the interests of the wealthy at the
expense of everyone else. It's not just about leopards and tariffs
anymore, it's about an entire system designed to keep the poor
as easy prey.

Part 2: A System Built to Prey

If tariffs are the leopard's teeth, then regressive taxation and
wealth inequality are its claws. Trump's tariffs weren't an
isolated policy failure, they were part of a much larger strategy,
one that has defined Republican economic policy for decades.
The GOP has mastered the art of spinning policies that reward
the rich as solutions for everyone else, often wrapped in patriotic
language or promises of trickle-down benefits. But when you
peel back the layers, you find the same consistent result: the
poor and working class carry the weight while the wealthiest
walk away unscathed, or better yet, richer than before. This is
the system we're living in, and it's been designed to keep
working people trapped in a cycle of struggling just to stay
afloat.

Let's start with taxes. The Trump administration's 2017 Tax
Cuts and Jobs Act was pitched as a win for the middle class, but
the reality was starkly different. Yes, many Americans saw
small, temporary tax cuts, but the biggest benefits were handed
to corporations and the wealthiest individuals. Corporate tax
rates were slashed from 35% to 21%, a historic drop that
primarily benefited large companies and their shareholders.
And those shareholders? They're overwhelmingly in the top 1%
of income earners. So, while working families got a little extra in
their paychecks for a few years, the richest Americans saw their
wealth skyrocket, and their tax breaks were permanent.

Here's the kicker: these tax cuts were never about creating jobs or boosting wages, despite what the GOP claimed. In fact, studies showed that the vast majority of the corporate windfall went to stock buybacks and dividends, moves that inflate stock prices and benefit investors, not workers. Meanwhile, ordinary Americans saw little to no improvement in their economic prospects. Wages remained stagnant, and income inequality continued to grow. The whole thing was a bait-and-switch, using the promise of middle-class relief to justify a massive giveaway to the rich.

But it didn't stop there. The tax cuts also blew a massive hole in the federal budget, $1.5 trillion over a decade, to be exact. And guess what happens when deficits balloon? Politicians start calling for cuts to social programs, the very safety nets that millions of low-income and working-class Americans rely on. This isn't a bug in the system; it's a feature. The GOP has long used deficits as a pretext to dismantle programs like Medicaid, food assistance, and Social Security, even though these programs are lifelines for the very people their policies harm the most.

The deregulation push during the Trump era followed the same pattern. Under the guise of "cutting red tape" and "freeing businesses to innovate," the administration rolled back environmental protections, worker safety standards, and consumer safeguards. These moves were often framed as helping small businesses and creating jobs, but the real beneficiaries were major corporations and their executives. For example, the rollback of regulations on pollution allowed industries like oil and gas to cut costs, but those savings didn't trickle down to workers or consumers. Instead, they went straight into the pockets of shareholders, while communities faced increased health risks and environmental degradation.

It's important to understand how these policies connect. Deregulation reduces costs for corporations, tax cuts boost their bottom line, and tariffs shift the financial burden to consumers.

Together, these policies create a feedback loop that concentrates wealth at the top while leaving everyone else to deal with the consequences. And the GOP has perfected the messaging to make it all seem inevitable, as though this is just the way the economy works. They frame any attempt to raise taxes on the rich or regulate big business as an attack on "job creators," even though there's little evidence to support that claim. It's a narrative that's been sold to the American people for decades, and it's been wildly successful, if you measure success by how much wealth the top 1% has accumulated.

Let's talk about that wealth gap for a moment because it's staggering. Over the past four decades, the share of wealth held by the top 1% has more than doubled, while the bottom 50% has seen its share shrink. During the Trump years, this trend accelerated. The combination of tax cuts, deregulation, and policies like tariffs made it easier than ever for the rich to get richer while everyone else struggled to keep up. And here's the thing: wealth inequality doesn't just hurt the poor, it destabilizes the entire economy. When so much wealth is concentrated at the top, consumer spending slows, economic growth stagnates, and opportunities for upward mobility disappear. It's like trying to run an engine on fumes while all the fuel is locked in one tank.

The housing crisis is another example of how these policies disproportionately harm low-income and working-class Americans. While Trump was touting economic growth, millions of Americans were being priced out of the housing market. Rising rents, stagnant wages, and cuts to affordable housing programs created a perfect storm for a crisis that hit the poorest families hardest. Meanwhile, wealthy investors were snapping up properties and driving up prices even further, profiting off the very instability that was pushing people out of their homes. It's a vicious cycle, and one that perfectly illustrates how GOP policies often exacerbate the very problems they claim to solve.

Even the pandemic didn't disrupt this pattern, it amplified it. While millions of Americans lost their jobs, struggled to pay rent, and lined up at food banks, the wealthiest Americans saw their fortunes grow exponentially. The stock market soared, fueled in part by government stimulus measures that disproportionately benefited corporations and the wealthy. The CARES Act, for example, included provisions that allowed businesses to claim massive tax refunds, even if they were profitable. At the same time, many small businesses struggled to access relief funds, and millions of workers were left out of unemployment benefits due to bureaucratic hurdles and state-level mismanagement. Once again, the leopard ate the poor, while the rich sat comfortably out of reach.

And then there's healthcare, or the lack of it. The Trump administration's attempts to dismantle the Affordable Care Act would have stripped millions of Americans of their health insurance, disproportionately affecting low-income families. Even without a full repeal, the administration's policies weakened the ACA, leading to higher premiums and fewer coverage options for those who needed it most. Meanwhile, pharmaceutical companies and healthcare conglomerates continued to rake in profits, shielded from accountability by a system designed to prioritize corporate interests over human lives.

What makes all of this even more infuriating is the rhetoric that accompanies it. Republicans often frame their policies as promoting "freedom" and "opportunity," but the reality is that these policies systematically limit both for the majority of Americans. When you can't afford healthcare, when your wages aren't enough to cover rent, when your job disappears because your employer couldn't compete with tariff-driven price hikes, that's not freedom. That's a rigged system designed to keep you running in place while the people at the top move further ahead.

As we transition into Part 3, we'll take a closer look at the broader cultural and political forces that enable this system to persist. It's not just about policies, it's about the narratives and ideologies that convince people to accept them, even when they're clearly harmful. We'll explore how the GOP has weaponized ideas like rugged individualism and self-reliance to justify policies that harm the very people they claim to protect. We'll also examine the role of corporate lobbying, media spin, and voter disenfranchisement in maintaining this cycle of inequality. The leopard isn't just eating the poor, it's been invited to the table, and it's time to figure out who set the place cards. Stay with me.

Part 3: Setting the Table for the Leopard

The leopard doesn't just wander in by chance, it's invited, fed, and allowed to feast by a system that's been carefully cultivated over decades. Republican policies, from tariffs to tax cuts, are one part of the equation, but the larger issue lies in the cultural narratives, political machinery, and corporate power structures that sustain this deeply unequal system. Why do leopards always eat the poor? Because the system has been built to ensure it. And even as the impacts of these policies disproportionately harm the most vulnerable, the mechanisms in place convince many of those affected to support, or at least tolerate, the very policies that keep them at the bottom of the table.

Let's start with the narrative of rugged individualism. For generations, Americans have been sold the idea that success is purely a result of personal effort, grit, and determination. The concept of the "self-made man" is baked into the national ethos, celebrated in everything from rags-to-riches tales to political speeches. But this narrative serves a specific purpose: it shifts responsibility for systemic failures away from the policymakers and corporations that create them and onto individuals who are told they simply didn't try hard enough. When tariffs raise the cost of goods, or when tax cuts for the wealthy drain funding

114

from public services, it's framed as a challenge to overcome rather than a structural problem to address. The leopard's claws are hidden behind the mantra of "personal responsibility."

This narrative is weaponized to justify policies that disproportionately harm the poor while rewarding the wealthy. For example, the idea that taxes are inherently bad or that government programs breed dependency is a common refrain in Republican rhetoric. By framing taxation as theft and social programs as handouts, the GOP creates a moral framework that positions wealth as a virtue and poverty as a personal failing. This ideology is incredibly effective because it appeals to both the aspirations of those who want to believe they, too, can become wealthy and the resentments of those who feel they're being forced to support others. It's the perfect smokescreen for policies that shift wealth upward.

Corporate lobbying plays a huge role in setting the leopard's table. Major industries spend billions every year influencing legislation, shaping public opinion, and ensuring that policies favor their bottom lines. During the Trump administration, corporations not only benefited from the massive tax cuts but also from deregulation that stripped away protections for workers, consumers, and the environment. These same corporations invest heavily in think tanks, media outlets, and advocacy groups that amplify pro-business, anti-regulation messages, further embedding these ideas into public discourse. When tariffs were imposed, for instance, the narrative pushed by many industry groups wasn't about protecting workers but about framing higher costs as a natural consequence of global competition, a problem for which workers, not executives, were expected to bear the burden.

The media plays its part as well. Corporate-owned outlets often present economic policies through a lens that prioritizes markets over people. Coverage of Trump's tax cuts, for example, often focused on stock market gains rather than the long-term implications for wage stagnation or inequality. When tariffs were implemented, much of the coverage emphasized the political drama or the impact on trade relationships rather than the day-to-day struggles of working families dealing with higher prices. This framing reinforces the idea that the health of the economy is synonymous with the health of the stock market, even though most Americans own little to no stock. Meanwhile, narratives about poverty and economic insecurity are often framed as personal struggles rather than systemic issues, perpetuating the myth that individuals are solely responsible for their circumstances.

Voter disenfranchisement is another tool in the leopard's arsenal. Policies like gerrymandering, voter ID laws, and restrictions on mail-in voting disproportionately affect low-income communities, people of color, and other marginalized groups, many of whom are the most directly harmed by Republican economic policies. By making it harder for these groups to vote, the GOP reduces the accountability that might otherwise challenge its agenda. The result is a feedback loop where the people most affected by regressive policies have less power to change them, while those who benefit maintain their influence.

The role of big money in politics cannot be overstated. The Citizens United decision, which allowed unlimited corporate spending in elections, has further tilted the playing field in favor of the wealthy and well-connected. Political campaigns are increasingly funded by billionaires and corporate interests, ensuring that candidates who support pro-business, anti-tax policies have the resources to dominate elections. This dynamic perpetuates a system where the interests of ordinary Americans are sidelined in favor of those with the deepest pockets. It's no wonder the leopard is so well-fed.

Even within Republican strongholds, the question arises: why do so many working-class and low-income voters support policies that hurt them? The answer lies in the GOP's ability to weaponize cultural issues and redirect economic frustrations toward scapegoats. Immigration, for example, is often framed as a threat to jobs and wages, even though the evidence shows that immigrants contribute far more to the economy than they take. Similarly, welfare programs are often depicted as rife with fraud and abuse, even though the majority of beneficiaries are children, the elderly, and the disabled. By stoking fears about "the other" and framing government programs as handouts to undeserving people, Republicans divert attention from the real beneficiaries of their policies: corporations and the ultra-wealthy.

This strategy also thrives on the polarization of political discourse. By framing Democrats as socialists or radicals, the GOP paints any attempt to address inequality or reform the tax system as an existential threat to freedom. This fear-mongering prevents meaningful dialogue about alternative economic policies and locks voters into a binary choice where any deviation from the status quo is seen as dangerous. It's a tactic designed to maintain the system as it is, with the leopard comfortably feasting on the poor.

Let's not forget the role of religion in this narrative. For decades, the Republican Party has aligned itself with evangelical Christianity, using moral arguments to justify economic policies that disproportionately harm the vulnerable. Prosperity gospel theology, which equates wealth with divine favor, has been particularly effective in reinforcing the idea that poverty is a sign of personal or spiritual failure. This ideology not only absolves the wealthy of responsibility for systemic inequality but also discourages collective action to address it, framing such efforts as attempts to undermine God's will.

The education system also plays a role in perpetuating inequality. Decades of underfunding public schools, particularly in low-income areas, have left millions of Americans without the tools to navigate or challenge the system. Meanwhile, wealthier families have access to private schools and well-funded public districts that prepare their children for success. This disparity creates a cycle where economic privilege is passed down through generations, while those without access to quality education remain trapped in low-paying jobs with little opportunity for advancement. The leopard eats, and the cycle continues.

As we wrap up this chapter, it's clear that the leopard isn't just a metaphor for the failures of Trump-era tariffs. It represents a much larger system, one that has been carefully constructed to prioritize the interests of the wealthy and powerful at the expense of everyone else. From tax cuts to deregulation, from voter suppression to media narratives, every piece of this puzzle is designed to keep the leopard fed. And while the GOP has mastered this strategy, it's not the only party complicit in maintaining the status quo. Changing this system will require more than just electing different leaders; it will require a fundamental shift in how we understand and approach economic policy.

Note: How Tariffs Help Other Countries More Than the U.S.

While tariffs are often sold as tools to bolster domestic industries and protect American workers, the reality is that they often end up benefiting other countries more than the United States. Here's how:

Driving Competitors to Other Markets: During the U.S.-China trade war, China retaliated with tariffs on U.S. agricultural exports, like soybeans. Brazil and Argentina seized the opportunity, capturing market share in China that U.S. farmers may never fully regain.

Incentivizing Supply Chain Diversification: Businesses moved operations to avoid U.S. tariffs, boosting economies like Vietnam, Malaysia, and Mexico, and weakening the U.S.'s central role in global trade.

Strengthening Geopolitical Alliances: As the U.S. alienated partners with tariffs, China expanded its Belt and Road Initiative, while the EU secured new trade deals, sidelining American businesses.

Increasing Competitiveness Against U.S. Exports: Retaliatory tariffs make U.S. goods less competitive abroad, allowing other countries, like Australia in beef markets, to dominate.

Encouraging Innovation Abroad: Higher costs for U.S. manufacturers reduce innovation, while countries outside the tariff zones, such as those in Southeast Asia, invest in efficiency and technology.

In essence, U.S. tariffs frequently backfire by unintentionally boosting the economic fortunes of other nations. They disrupt long-standing trade relationships, force businesses to look for alternatives, and give competing countries the chance to step in and fill the void. The result? A less competitive U.S. economy and a world where the supposed beneficiaries of tariffs, American workers and businesses, are left watching others reap the rewards.

Note: But What About Biden (in a Whiny Both-Sides Voice) Didn't He Keep Trump's Tariffs Because They're Sooooo Good?

Yes, President Biden has kept many of Trump's tariffs in place, but it's not because he's suddenly a convert to the Church of Tariff-Waving Economic Brilliance. The truth is far messier, and decidedly less flattering for those who argue that Trump's tariffs were a stroke of policy genius. Biden inherited not a set of meticulously crafted economic tools but a tangled web of trade wars, supply chain disruptions, and fractured alliances. Dismantling the mess overnight would risk even more chaos in an already precarious economic landscape. So yes, the tariffs remain, but not as a testament to their perfection, they're a pragmatic, temporary holdover in service of a much broader, more strategic approach.

Let's get one thing straight: Biden's decision to keep many of Trump's tariffs doesn't mean he's singing their praises. Far from it. The reality is that reversing tariffs is not like flipping a switch; it's more like diffusing a bomb. A sudden rollback could destabilize industries that have grudgingly adapted to the tariffs and further exacerbate economic tensions with China. Instead, Biden is using the tariffs as leverage to tackle systemic issues, things like intellectual property theft, forced technology transfers, and labor abuses, challenges that existed long before Trump and that require far more than blunt economic tools to address.

Unlike Trump, who treated tariffs as a centerpiece of his nationalist rhetoric, Biden's strategy is less about chest-thumping and more about steady, calculated moves. The Biden administration has reframed the tariffs not as weapons in a zero-sum trade war but as tools in a broader diplomatic and economic strategy. This approach reflects a shift from Trump's performative bravado to a more nuanced effort to rebuild alliances, stabilize global trade, and address the systemic imbalances that Trump's go-it-alone tactics ignored, or worsened.

For example, Biden has prioritized working with allies to counter China's economic influence, moving away from Trump's isolating tactics. Rather than alienating key trading partners with unilateral tariffs, the administration has pursued collaborative strategies, aiming to create a unified front against unfair practices. This shift in tone and strategy highlights a fundamental difference: Trump's tariffs were wielded like sledgehammers to reinforce his America First rhetoric, while Biden is using them like scaffolding, holding up an imperfect structure while working on something more durable and inclusive.

Critics who claim that Biden's retention of tariffs validates their success conveniently ignore the complexities of trade policy. For one, the economic disruptions caused by Trump's tariffs didn't just evaporate after his term ended. Supply chains were upended, industries adjusted (often at great cost), and international relations were strained. Abruptly removing the tariffs now could amplify these disruptions, undercutting American businesses and workers who've spent years navigating this new reality. Biden's approach acknowledges these realities, using the tariffs not as a permanent solution but as a temporary tool to manage the fallout of Trump's chaotic trade policies.

The situation underscores an important distinction between the two administrations. Trump's tariffs were performative, driven by nationalist rhetoric and short-term political calculus. Biden, on the other hand, has taken a more deliberate approach, using the existing tariffs to buy time and create leverage for systemic changes. This isn't an endorsement of Trump's policies, it's damage control. And damage control isn't about celebrating the status quo; it's about making the best of a bad hand while working toward a better one.

Take the issue of China, for instance. Trump's tariffs were part of an erratic trade war that did little to address the structural issues in U.S.-China relations. Intellectual property theft, forced labor, and market access barriers didn't magically disappear because Trump slapped tariffs on Chinese goods. Instead, his unilateral approach alienated allies and left the U.S. grappling with retaliatory measures and higher costs for consumers and businesses. Biden's approach, by contrast, involves reengaging with allies to tackle these challenges collectively. By building a coalition of nations with shared concerns about China's economic practices, the administration is working toward a more coordinated and effective strategy, one that uses tariffs as a tool, not as an end in itself.

Another key difference is the way the tariffs are being positioned domestically. Under Trump, tariffs were sold as a patriotic crusade to protect American workers and industries, even as their regressive impacts disproportionately hurt low-income households and small businesses. Biden's administration has been more candid about the limitations of tariffs, framing them as temporary measures rather than silver bullets. This transparency is crucial for shifting the narrative away from economic nationalism and toward a more honest conversation about the trade-offs and complexities of global trade.

Of course, this doesn't mean Biden's approach is without its flaws. The decision to keep the tariffs in place has drawn criticism from multiple sides, with some arguing that it signals a lack of ambition to tackle the root causes of economic inequality. Others contend that the tariffs continue to burden American consumers and businesses, particularly those in industries heavily reliant on imports. These criticisms are valid, but they also highlight the challenges of governing in the wake of Trump's chaos. Trade policy is a long game, and undoing years of disruption requires patience, pragmatism, and an eye toward systemic reform.

Biden's administration has also sought to mitigate the regressive effects of tariffs through domestic investments and social programs. Initiatives like the Inflation Reduction Act and infrastructure spending aim to create jobs, reduce costs for families, and strengthen industries that have been left vulnerable by decades of disinvestment. These measures, while not directly tied to trade policy, reflect a broader effort to build an economy that is more resilient and equitable, a stark contrast to Trump's focus on symbolic gestures that often benefited the wealthy at the expense of everyone else.

So, does Biden's retention of Trump's tariffs mean they were "good"? Hardly. What it does mean is that trade policy is complicated, and the consequences of bad decisions don't disappear when a new administration takes over. Biden's approach is less about validating tariffs as an ideal and more about managing their fallout while pursuing longer-term goals. It's an acknowledgment that trade wars don't end with a single stroke of a pen; they require careful unwinding, strategic planning, and an honest reckoning with the damage already done.

Ultimately, Biden's use of tariffs highlights the difference between symbolic policymaking and practical governance. Trump's tariffs were a show of strength, designed to rally his base and project an image of toughness. Biden's approach, by contrast, reflects a deeper understanding of the complexities of trade and the interconnectedness of global economies. It's not flashy, and it's certainly not perfect, but it's a step toward a more thoughtful and effective trade strategy, one that prioritizes stability, collaboration, and the long-term health of the economy over short-term political gains.

In the end, the retention of tariffs under Biden is less about what Trump got right and more about what he got wrong. It's a reminder that cleaning up the mess left by performative policies takes time, effort, and a willingness to learn from past mistakes. And while tariffs may remain part of the toolbox for now, the ultimate goal is to build a system where they're no longer necessary, a system that values fairness, sustainability, and shared prosperity over the empty promises of economic nationalism. If anything, the ongoing use of tariffs under Biden underscores the importance of moving beyond them, toward a trade policy that works for everyone, not just the leopards.

Chapter 9
Patriotic Leopards – The Big Lie

Part 1: The Illusion of Patriotic Sacrifice

Trump's use of patriotism to sell tariffs was as calculated as it was effective. By framing tariffs as a tool to protect American jobs and revive the nation's industrial heartland, he tapped into deeply rooted feelings of economic insecurity and cultural pride. In speeches and rallies, he painted a vivid picture of a nation under siege, foreign competitors exploiting American generosity, factories rusting away in forgotten towns, and working-class families losing their livelihoods to global forces beyond their control. Against this backdrop, tariffs were presented not just as economic policy but as an act of patriotic defiance, a way for Americans to "fight back" against those who would undermine the nation's greatness.

The appeal of this message was undeniable. For many rural and working-class Americans, particularly in regions hardest hit by deindustrialization, the promise of tariffs offered a lifeline. Here was a president who seemed to see their struggles, who spoke directly to their pain and promised to do something about it. But this narrative, powerful as it was, rested on a foundation of half-truths and outright lies. Far from being a solution to the challenges facing these communities, tariffs often exacerbated their problems, imposing costs that fell disproportionately on those least able to bear them.

Take, for example, the steel and aluminum tariffs of 2018. Trump frequently cited these measures as evidence of his commitment to American workers, claiming they would revitalize domestic production and restore the nation's industrial might. In the short term, there were indeed some visible successes, steel mills reopened, and a modest number of jobs were created in the sector. These achievements were celebrated in presidential tweets and campaign speeches, held up as proof that the tariffs were working. But this victory lap ignored the broader picture.

For every job saved or created in the steel industry, several were lost in downstream industries like automotive manufacturing, construction, and appliances, which rely on steel and aluminum as key inputs. These industries faced skyrocketing costs, forcing them to make difficult choices, laying off workers, delaying projects, or passing the increased costs onto consumers. The ripple effects of these decisions were felt across the economy, undermining the very goals the tariffs were supposed to achieve.

In rural communities, the impact of Trump's trade war was even more pronounced. China, the primary target of Trump's tariffs, responded with retaliatory measures that hit American agriculture particularly hard. Soybean farmers, who had relied on China as their largest export market, saw demand evaporate almost overnight. Prices plummeted, leaving farmers with unsold crops and mounting debt. While the federal government attempted to mitigate these losses with bailout programs, the aid was often poorly targeted and insufficient to cover the damage. Large agribusinesses fared better, but small family farms, already struggling to compete in an increasingly consolidated industry, were pushed to the brink.

The irony of this situation was hard to miss. The very people who had been held up as symbols of American resilience and self-reliance, rural farmers and industrial workers, were now paying the price for policies that claimed to protect them. Yet, the rhetoric of patriotism continued unabated, shielding these policies from scrutiny and deflecting blame onto external enemies.

Trump's framing of tariffs as an act of patriotic sacrifice also played on deeply ingrained narratives about American exceptionalism and self-reliance. By buying into this narrative, many Americans were willing to accept short-term pain in the hope of long-term gain. Farmers who saw their livelihoods collapse under the weight of retaliatory tariffs were told to "hang in there" because they were part of a larger battle for economic justice. Factory workers who lost their jobs because their employers couldn't absorb higher input costs were reassured that their sacrifices were necessary to "level the playing field."

This narrative of sacrifice was not new. Throughout history, political leaders have used patriotic appeals to justify policies that disproportionately benefit the wealthy and powerful while imposing costs on the poor and working class. During World War II, for example, the U.S. government framed wage freezes and rationing as acts of patriotic duty, even as corporations reaped massive profits from wartime production. In the 1980s, Ronald Reagan invoked the language of patriotism to sell tax cuts for the wealthy and deregulation for corporations, arguing that these measures would unleash the "magic of the marketplace" and restore America's greatness.

What sets Trump apart is the brazenness with which he exploited these narratives. By wrapping his tariff policies in the flag, he not only obscured their true costs but also weaponized patriotism against dissent. Those who criticized the tariffs were cast as un-American, accused of siding with foreign competitors or undermining the president's efforts to protect the nation. This framing created a climate of fear and conformity, where legitimate concerns about the economic and social impacts of tariffs were drowned out by the roar of patriotic fervor.

The manipulation of patriotism to sell tariffs also relied on a selective reading of history. Trump frequently invoked the legacy of past protectionist policies, such as the tariffs of the 19th century, as evidence that his approach was rooted in tradition and common sense. What he failed to acknowledge was the context in which these policies were implemented. In the 19th century, tariffs were one of the primary sources of government revenue, used to fund infrastructure projects and promote industrial development in a largely agrarian economy. By contrast, the modern economy is deeply interconnected, with global supply chains and complex trade relationships that make the blanket application of tariffs far more disruptive.

Moreover, the historical record shows that protectionist policies often produced mixed results. While they may have provided short-term benefits to certain industries, they also contributed to economic inefficiencies, trade imbalances, and international tensions. The Smoot-Hawley Tariff Act of 1930, for example, is widely regarded as a policy disaster, exacerbating the Great Depression by stifling global trade and provoking retaliatory measures from other countries. By cherry-picking examples from history, Trump crafted a narrative that ignored these complexities, presenting tariffs as a one-size-fits-all solution to the challenges of globalization.

As this chapter moves into Part 2, we will explore how the manipulation of patriotism to sell tariffs fits into a broader pattern of political propaganda and economic exploitation. From the use of fear-mongering to the deliberate misrepresentation of policy impacts, we will examine the tools and tactics that leaders use to manipulate public opinion and advance their own agendas. By understanding these dynamics, we can begin to unravel the myths that sustain harmful policies and chart a path toward a more equitable and transparent approach to economic governance.

Part 2: Manipulation Through Patriotism – A Historical Playbook

The exploitation of patriotism to advance policies that disproportionately harm the vulnerable is not unique to Trump. His use of tariffs as a rallying cry for economic nationalism fits into a broader historical pattern of leveraging national pride to obscure the true beneficiaries of political decisions. Whether through the language of sacrifice or the demonization of external enemies, this strategy has been deployed time and again to shift focus away from the inequities of economic systems and onto symbolic displays of loyalty. To understand Trump's approach to tariffs, it's essential to examine how this playbook has been used throughout history to manipulate public sentiment and entrench systems of inequality.

One of the most prominent examples of this manipulation can be found in the New Deal era. Franklin D. Roosevelt's administration, while often celebrated for its progressive reforms, also relied on patriotic appeals to rally public support for policies that had mixed outcomes for different social groups. Programs like the Agricultural Adjustment Act (AAA) promised to stabilize the farming economy but often did so at the expense of tenant farmers and sharecroppers, disproportionately impacting African Americans in the South. These sacrifices were framed as necessary for the greater good, with patriotic rhetoric masking the unequal distribution of benefits and burdens.

Similarly, during World War II, the U.S. government used patriotic propaganda to justify policies that demanded significant sacrifices from working-class Americans while allowing corporations to profit handsomely from wartime production. Wage freezes and rationing were sold as acts of national duty, while industries like steel, oil, and aviation reaped the rewards of lucrative government contracts. This dynamic is strikingly similar to Trump's tariff policies, which imposed higher costs on consumers and small businesses while protecting the profits of large corporations in select industries.

Fast-forward to the Reagan era, and the pattern becomes even clearer. Reagan's tax cuts and deregulation initiatives were couched in the language of American exceptionalism and entrepreneurial spirit, portraying them as steps toward unleashing the full potential of the nation's economy. In reality, these policies primarily benefited the wealthy, exacerbating income inequality and undermining social safety nets. By framing these measures as patriotic, Reagan deflected criticism and silenced dissent, creating a political environment in which questioning the wisdom of his policies was equated with questioning the values of the nation itself.

Trump's tariffs fit neatly into this tradition. By invoking the language of patriotism, he shifted attention away from the economic realities of his policies and toward an emotional narrative of national revival. This narrative was particularly effective in rural and industrial communities, where years of economic decline had left many feeling abandoned and ignored. By positioning tariffs as a tool to "bring back" jobs and industries, Trump tapped into a deep well of resentment and frustration, offering a sense of purpose and agency to those who felt left behind by globalization.

However, this narrative was built on a series of distortions. For one, it ignored the structural factors driving economic decline in these regions, such as automation, corporate consolidation, and decades of disinvestment in education and infrastructure. Tariffs, no matter how aggressive, could do little to address these underlying issues. Instead, they functioned as a symbolic gesture, a way to create the appearance of action without delivering meaningful change.

The manipulation of patriotism also relied heavily on the demonization of external enemies. Just as Reagan framed the Soviet Union as the "Evil Empire" to justify his military spending, Trump used China as a scapegoat to rally support for his trade policies. By portraying China as a malevolent force intent on undermining American prosperity, he created a sense of urgency and solidarity that obscured the real costs of his tariffs. This tactic was particularly effective in rural areas, where the impacts of globalization were often most visible and where skepticism of foreign powers ran deep.

Yet, the narrative of China as the ultimate villain in the story of American economic decline was deeply flawed. While China's trade practices, including intellectual property theft and market manipulation, have undoubtedly created challenges for the U.S., they are far from the sole cause of economic hardship in rural and industrial communities. By focusing exclusively on China, Trump diverted attention from domestic policies and corporate behaviors that have contributed to these struggles. For example, the offshoring of jobs by American companies, driven by a desire to maximize profits, played a far greater role in the decline of manufacturing than any single trade agreement or foreign competitor.

The selective use of history was another key element of Trump's patriotic narrative. By invoking the legacy of past protectionist policies, he presented tariffs as a time-tested solution to the challenges of globalization. However, this historical framing ignored the mixed results of these policies. While tariffs in the 19th century did protect emerging industries, they also created inefficiencies and trade imbalances that hindered long-term economic growth. Moreover, the global context has changed dramatically since then, with supply chains and trade relationships far more interconnected than they were in the era of high tariffs.

The consequences of Trump's manipulation of patriotism to sell tariffs extended far beyond economic policy. By framing his trade war as a battle for the soul of the nation, he deepened divisions both domestically and internationally. At home, his rhetoric pitted different groups of Americans against each other, with farmers and steelworkers cast as heroes while critics of the tariffs were labeled unpatriotic. This polarization made it difficult to build consensus around alternative approaches to trade policy, leaving the nation mired in conflict and stagnation.

Internationally, Trump's patriotic appeals alienated key allies and undermined the multilateral institutions that have traditionally facilitated global trade. Countries that had long seen the U.S. as a reliable partner were blindsided by the sudden imposition of tariffs, leading to retaliatory measures and a breakdown of trust. This erosion of goodwill not only weakened America's position in the global economy but also created openings for rivals like China to expand their influence.

As this chapter moves into Part 3, we will examine how Trump's use of patriotism to sell tariffs fits into a broader pattern of economic exploitation and political propaganda. By exploring the ways in which leaders manipulate public sentiment to advance their agendas, we can begin to unravel the myths that sustain harmful policies and chart a path toward a more equitable and transparent approach to governance. The story of Trump's tariffs is not just a cautionary tale about the dangers of economic nationalism, it is also a call to action, a reminder that true patriotism lies in holding leaders accountable and demanding policies that serve the common good.

Part 3: Unmasking Patriotism's Exploitation

The final piece of Trump's manipulation of patriotism to sell his tariff policies lies in its broader implications for economic exploitation and political propaganda. While the narrative of national pride and economic independence resonated deeply with many Americans, it served as a smokescreen for policies that entrenched inequality and rewarded the very elites that Trump's rhetoric claimed to oppose. This bait-and-switch, using patriotic appeals to mask the enrichment of the wealthy and the marginalization of the working class, has deep historical roots but reached new levels of brazenness during Trump's presidency.

Central to this manipulation was the idea of loyalty. Trump's rhetoric framed the trade war as a test of allegiance: either you stood with his administration's tariffs, or you sided with foreign powers that sought to exploit American workers. This binary choice left little room for nuance or debate, forcing Americans to accept policies that harmed their own economic interests in the name of patriotism. For rural farmers facing bankruptcy or small business owners grappling with skyrocketing costs, voicing opposition to tariffs became tantamount to betraying their country. This environment of fear and conformity stifled critical discourse, allowing harmful policies to proceed unchecked.

But loyalty, as Trump framed it, was a one-way street. While ordinary Americans were called upon to make sacrifices for the supposed greater good, corporate interests and wealthy elites were reaping the rewards of the administration's policies. The tariffs on Chinese goods, for instance, created opportunities for multinational corporations to shift production to other low-cost countries, circumventing the very measures that were meant to protect American industry. Meanwhile, consumers faced higher prices for everything from electronics to clothing, effectively subsidizing corporate profits through their purchases.

This dynamic mirrors a long history of economic exploitation disguised as patriotism. During the Gilded Age, industrialists wrapped their anti-labor practices in the language of national progress, claiming that strikes and unionization efforts threatened America's economic growth. In the post-war era, the rise of suburbanization and consumer culture was often framed as a patriotic duty, even as it deepened racial and economic divides. And in the Reagan years, the rollback of social safety nets was justified by appeals to individual responsibility and free-market values, leaving millions of Americans to fend for themselves in an increasingly unequal society.

Trump's tariffs followed this same pattern. While they were presented as a tool to protect American workers and industries, their primary beneficiaries were the wealthy and well-connected. Industries like steel and aluminum, which received direct protection from the tariffs, saw short-term gains that disproportionately benefited corporate executives and shareholders. At the same time, the broader economy absorbed the costs of these measures, with downstream industries, small businesses, and consumers bearing the brunt of the fallout.

The federal bailout programs for farmers, totaling $28 billion, provide a stark example of how this dynamic played out. While these programs were ostensibly designed to support struggling agricultural communities, much of the aid went to large agribusinesses with the resources to weather the trade war. Small family farms, which lacked the capital and scale to compete, often found themselves excluded from these benefits or receiving payouts that barely covered their losses. This uneven distribution of resources deepened existing inequalities within the agricultural sector, further consolidating power in the hands of a few large players.

Internationally, Trump's tariffs weakened America's standing in the global economy while strengthening the position of its rivals. The trade war with China, far from curbing Beijing's influence, prompted the Chinese government to accelerate its efforts to diversify its trade relationships and expand its economic footprint. Initiatives like the Belt and Road Initiative gained traction as China positioned itself as a more reliable partner for countries disillusioned by America's unilateralism. At the same time, traditional allies like Canada, Mexico, and the European Union forged new trade agreements that excluded the U.S., reducing its leverage in global negotiations.

Domestically, the rhetoric of patriotic sacrifice masked a deeper truth: Trump's tariffs were part of a broader Republican agenda that systematically prioritized the interests of the wealthy over those of ordinary Americans. From the 2017 tax cuts, which disproportionately benefited corporations and high-income earners, to the rollback of environmental and labor regulations, the administration's policies consistently shifted power and resources upward. The tariffs fit neatly into this framework, creating the illusion of economic justice while perpetuating a system that exacerbated inequality.

The social and psychological impacts of this exploitation are profound. For many Americans, particularly those in rural and industrial communities, the promise of tariffs represented a rare moment of hope, a chance to reclaim agency in a system that had long seemed stacked against them. When these promises went unfulfilled, the resulting disillusionment deepened feelings of mistrust and alienation. This erosion of faith in government institutions created fertile ground for conspiracy theories and extremist ideologies, further polarizing the political landscape and undermining the potential for collective action.

What makes Trump's use of patriotism particularly dangerous is its weaponization of identity. By framing economic policy as a moral and cultural battle, he tapped into the anxieties of a nation grappling with rapid change and uncertainty. This strategy was highly effective in rallying support but came at a steep cost. The rhetoric of "America First" not only alienated allies and trading partners but also reinforced a zero-sum mindset that pitted Americans against each other. Workers in industries seen as beneficiaries of tariffs, like steel and aluminum, were celebrated as patriots, while those in industries harmed by the policies, like agriculture and retail, were cast as collateral damage. This division obscured the systemic nature of the challenges facing the U.S. economy, creating a fragmented and adversarial political environment.

The lessons of Trump's tariffs are clear: patriotism, when wielded as a political weapon, becomes a tool of exploitation rather than empowerment. By wrapping harmful policies in the language of national pride, leaders can deflect criticism, suppress dissent, and entrench systems of inequality. But unmasking this manipulation requires more than simply identifying its tactics, it demands a commitment to building a more inclusive and equitable vision of patriotism, one that celebrates shared values rather than exploiting divisions.

As this chapter concludes, it is worth reflecting on what true patriotism looks like in the context of economic policy. It is not blind allegiance to policies that harm the vulnerable or enrich the powerful. Nor is it the demonization of foreign competitors or dissenting voices. True patriotism lies in the pursuit of policies that promote fairness, equity, and collective well-being. It lies in holding leaders accountable for their decisions and demanding transparency and accountability in governance. And it lies in the recognition that the strength of a nation is measured not by the wealth of its elites but by the dignity and prosperity of its people.

In the end, the story of Trump's tariffs is not just a cautionary tale about the dangers of economic nationalism. It is a reminder of the power of narrative and the need to reclaim patriotism from those who would use it as a shield for exploitation. By challenging the myths that sustain harmful policies, we can begin to build an economy, and a nation, that truly works for everyone.

Conclusion
Leopards Always Win – If We Let Them

Part 1: How Leopards Feast Now and Will Feast Again

Trump's first term showed us exactly how leopards feast on the people who trust them. His tariffs, sold as bold patriotism and economic strength, disproportionately hurt working-class Americans while enriching the already wealthy. Now, with his second administration looming, the leopards are sharpening their claws, ready to pounce again with an expanded menu of proposed tariffs and trade policies. If history is any guide, the pain felt in his first term will pale in comparison to what's coming.

The tariffs imposed during Trump's first administration were framed as a defense of American workers and industries. They were pitched as a way to stop the erosion of manufacturing jobs, counteract unfair trade practices, and restore the glory of America's industrial past. But for millions of Americans, the reality was far grimmer. Tariffs on steel, aluminum, and Chinese imports led to higher costs for businesses and consumers, creating a cascade of economic strain that rippled through communities. Workers were laid off, small businesses struggled to stay afloat, and low-income households paid more for essentials like groceries and appliances.

As the Trump administration prepares to double down on its "America First" trade rhetoric, the proposed tariffs for the upcoming term promise to repeat, and amplify, these patterns. Promises of revitalized industries will resurface, but the policies themselves will once again function as regressive taxes. Tariffs on foreign goods will drive up prices for everyday items, disproportionately affecting those who can least afford them. Families already grappling with inflation and stagnant wages will face even greater financial insecurity. For the wealthy, however, the story will remain the same: tax cuts, deregulation, and financial loopholes will ensure that the leopards' feast is as bountiful as ever.

In Trump's proposed second-term trade agenda, we see a vision of economic isolationism that ignores the realities of global supply chains and interdependence. Higher tariffs on foreign goods, expanded to include an even broader range of imports, will push businesses into impossible corners. Small and medium-sized enterprises, already operating on thin margins, will bear the brunt of these policies. Retailers dependent on affordable imports will face skyrocketing costs, leaving them with little choice but to raise prices, cut staff, or close altogether. These closures won't just hurt employees; they'll devastate local economies, hollowing out communities that are already struggling to survive.

The agricultural sector, which was battered by Trump's first round of trade wars, is unlikely to fare better in the second term. Farmers, promised that tariffs would protect their livelihoods, instead saw critical export markets evaporate when countries like China retaliated with tariffs of their own. The government's bailout programs offered some relief, but these funds disproportionately flowed to large agribusinesses, leaving smaller farms to face bankruptcy. The second wave of tariffs is poised to repeat this pattern, cutting off access to international markets while failing to provide meaningful support for family farms.

What's worse, Trump's proposed tariffs are already prompting retaliation before they've even been enacted. Major trading partners, wary of the economic chaos wrought during his first term, are preparing their own measures to shield themselves from the fallout. This tit-for-tat dynamic will not only harm American exporters but will also weaken the U.S.'s standing in global trade networks. The trust and cooperation needed to navigate an interconnected economy will erode further, isolating the U.S. and leaving it vulnerable to economic shocks.

The social consequences of these policies will be devastating. Rural and working-class communities, already suffering from years of neglect and economic decline, will once again be sold false promises of renewal. When these promises inevitably go unfulfilled, the disillusionment will deepen, fostering resentment and mistrust. Divisions between industries, regions, and socioeconomic groups will widen as the narrative of "winners" and "losers" plays out yet again. Steelworkers might be portrayed as beneficiaries of the tariffs, while farmers and consumers bear the costs, fueling animosity and undermining solidarity.

The political implications of this disillusionment are equally troubling. As people struggle to make sense of why their financial burdens keep increasing, the rhetoric of scapegoating will intensify. Immigrants, foreign governments, and even fellow Americans will be blamed for the failures of these policies, creating a fertile ground for political polarization and extremism. The leopards know that division serves their interests; as long as people are fighting one another, they won't notice who's really eating their faces.

Trump's second-term tariff agenda also promises to accelerate the consolidation of wealth and power. By driving up costs for small businesses and consumers, these policies will create opportunities for large corporations to dominate markets even further. Multinational conglomerates, with the resources to navigate complex trade environments, will absorb smaller competitors, reducing competition and choice. For workers, this consolidation means fewer job opportunities, weaker bargaining power, and lower wages. For consumers, it means higher prices and diminished access to essential goods and services.

Meanwhile, the wealthiest Americans will continue to benefit from the very policies that harm everyone else. Corporate tax cuts and deregulation will ensure that the leopards at the top keep their claws sharp and their bellies full. The financial windfalls from these policies won't trickle down to workers or small businesses; they'll be funneled into stock buybacks, executive bonuses, and offshore accounts. The gap between the rich and everyone else will widen, perpetuating the cycle of inequality that has come to define the American economy.

As we stand on the brink of Trump's second term, the stakes couldn't be higher. The leopards are poised to feast on the same communities they've devoured before, and their appetite has only grown. But this isn't just a story about what will happen if these policies are implemented. It's also a story about what could happen if we choose a different path. Part 2 will explore the steps we can take to break the cycle, challenge the leopards, and create an economy that works for everyone. The future isn't set in stone, but it will require courage, accountability, and solidarity to ensure that the leopards don't win again.

Part 2: How to Stop Feeding the Leopards

If Trump's first term showed us how leopards feast, and his looming second term promises an even larger buffet, it's clear that the only way to stop the leopards is to stop feeding them. This means rejecting the policies that allow them to thrive and replacing them with economic strategies that prioritize fairness, sustainability, and collective prosperity. It also requires challenging the narratives that have enabled their rise, narratives of economic nationalism, unregulated capitalism, and the false promise that the wealth of the few will somehow benefit the many.

The first step in stopping the leopards is to recognize the systemic nature of their feeding frenzy. Trump's tariffs were not isolated missteps; they were part of a broader pattern of policies that funnel wealth and power upward while leaving the majority to struggle. Regressive tax cuts, deregulation, and the erosion of labor protections have all played a role in creating an economy that works for the few at the expense of the many. To reverse this trend, we need policies that address these systemic imbalances head-on, starting with the tax code.

A fairer tax system would ensure that the wealthiest Americans and corporations pay their share, closing the loopholes and offshore havens that allow them to hoard resources while the rest of the country bears the burden. This includes taxing capital gains at the same rate as income, introducing a wealth tax on billionaires, and implementing corporate minimum taxes to prevent profitable companies from avoiding their obligations. These measures wouldn't just generate revenue for public investment; they'd also signal a commitment to economic justice, challenging the idea that the richest among us are untouchable.

Labor protections must also be a cornerstone of any strategy to stop the leopards. For decades, the decline of unions and collective bargaining power has left workers vulnerable to exploitation, stagnant wages, and unsafe conditions. Strengthening labor laws to protect organizing efforts, penalize union-busting, and ensure fair wages and benefits is essential for leveling the playing field. When workers have a voice and a seat at the table, they can demand a fair share of the wealth they help create, making it harder for leopards to feast unchecked.

Investing in public goods is another crucial step in breaking the cycle. Decades of disinvestment in education, infrastructure, and healthcare have created a landscape where opportunity is scarce and economic mobility is stagnant. By prioritizing funding for public schools, vocational training programs, and affordable higher education, we can equip people with the skills they need to thrive in a rapidly changing economy. Modernizing infrastructure, from roads and bridges to broadband and renewable energy, can create jobs, improve productivity, and lay the foundation for sustainable growth. And ensuring access to affordable healthcare and childcare can alleviate some of the financial pressures that make households vulnerable to economic shocks.

Trade policy must also be reimagined to reflect the realities of a globalized economy while protecting workers and communities. This means moving away from unilateral tariffs and toward collaborative trade agreements that include enforceable labor and environmental standards. Agreements like the revised TPP (had it been renegotiated rather than abandoned) could serve as models for creating partnerships that prioritize equity and sustainability over corporate profits. These agreements should include mechanisms for supporting workers displaced by trade, such as retraining programs and wage subsidies, to ensure that the benefits of globalization are shared more broadly.

Challenging the leopards also requires confronting the narratives that have enabled their rise. For too long, economic nationalism has been wielded as a weapon to distract from systemic inequality. The rhetoric of "America First" suggests that the country's problems can be solved by isolating itself from the rest of the world, but this ignores the interconnected nature of modern economies. The reality is that global challenges require global solutions, and collaboration, not isolation, is the key to addressing issues like climate change, supply chain resilience, and technological innovation.

Similarly, the myth of the "self-made man" has been used to justify policies that reward the wealthy and punish the poor. This narrative obscures the role of collective effort, public investment, and systemic privilege in creating opportunities for success. Reframing the conversation around economic achievement to emphasize the importance of community, equity, and shared responsibility can help dismantle the cultural underpinnings of policies that favor the few over the many.

Stopping the leopards also means holding them accountable for the damage they've already done. This includes robust antitrust enforcement to break up monopolies and restore competition in key industries, from tech to agriculture to healthcare. It also means investigating and addressing the corporate corruption and political influence that have allowed leopards to rig the system in their favor. Transparency and accountability are essential for restoring public trust and ensuring that future policies serve the public good rather than private interests.

At the community level, organizing and advocacy are critical for building resistance to the leopards' agenda. Grassroots movements, unions, and advocacy groups have the power to push back against harmful policies and demand better from elected officials. By mobilizing voters, raising awareness, and building coalitions across industries and demographics, these movements can create the pressure needed to enact meaningful change.

Finally, stopping the leopards requires a commitment to long-term thinking. Policies that prioritize short-term political gains over sustainable solutions are what allowed the leopards to thrive in the first place. A forward-looking approach that invests in resilience, adaptability, and equity can ensure that the economy works for everyone, not just those at the top. This includes preparing for the economic disruptions of the future, from automation to climate change, by investing in research, innovation, and social safety nets that protect the most vulnerable.

The leopards have feasted for far too long, but their reign is not inevitable. By challenging the policies and narratives that enable them, we can create an economy that prioritizes fairness, justice, and sustainability. It won't be easy, and it won't happen overnight, but the alternative, allowing the leopards to keep winning, is simply too costly. The time to act is now, before the leopards' appetite becomes insatiable and the damage they've done becomes irreversible. If we want to stop the leopards, we have to stop feeding them, and start building a system that works for everyone.

List of Prints

About EATMS Productions

What's happening to women now is not random. It's structural.

Policy, culture, technology, and power are moving in the same direction.

EATMS maps them clearly and shows how to respond.

This title is part of an ongoing body of work. All EATMS Productions titles, across all series, authors, and formats, are components of a single connected project.

Start here: EATMS System Primer — Free Bundle
https://eatms.gumroad.com/l/dyvzbw

For full catalog or inquiries: eatms.me

Free survival booklet + EATMS updates: email "EATMS" to eatms@pm.me

Please feel free to burn part or all of this book, safely, as an effigy.